English ⌗ Heritage

Book of
The Tower of London

English # Heritage

Book of
The Tower of London

Geoffrey Parnell

B. T. Batsford Ltd/English Heritage
London

First published 1993

Typeset by Goodfellow & Egan Ltd., Cambridge
and printed in Great Britain by
The Bath Press, Avon

Published by B T Batsford Ltd
4 Fitzhardinge Street, London W1H 0AH

A CIP catalogue record for this book is
available from the British Library

ISBN 0 7134 6863 7 (cased)
ISBN 0 7134 6864 5 (limp)

Contents

Illustrations

Colour plates

Acknowledgements

I should like to record my particular gratitude to Peter Curnow, former Principal Inspector of Ancient Monuments, for all the considerable help and encouragement he has given over the years, without which this book could never have been written. My colleague, Terry Ball, Head of Section in English Heritage's Survey Unit, not only provided the reconstruction drawings, but must be credited with a great number of discoveries and observations made during the course of recording the Tower over many years. Jeremy Hall, Senior Photographer at the Royal Armouries, who has also provided a grand service at the Tower over a long period of time, is thanked for all his valuable help and assistance with the illustrative material.

Sarah Barter-Bailey, Librarian at the Royal Armouries, has been most generous with information and ideas. Christine Boddington, Andy McLaren and Peter Dunn of English Heritage's Illustrator's Office patiently reworked my site plans and David Honour of the Royal Palaces Agency produced **54**. Finally, I am grateful to Stephen Johnson for reading the draft text and making various amendments and offering useful advice, needless to say any errors are my own.

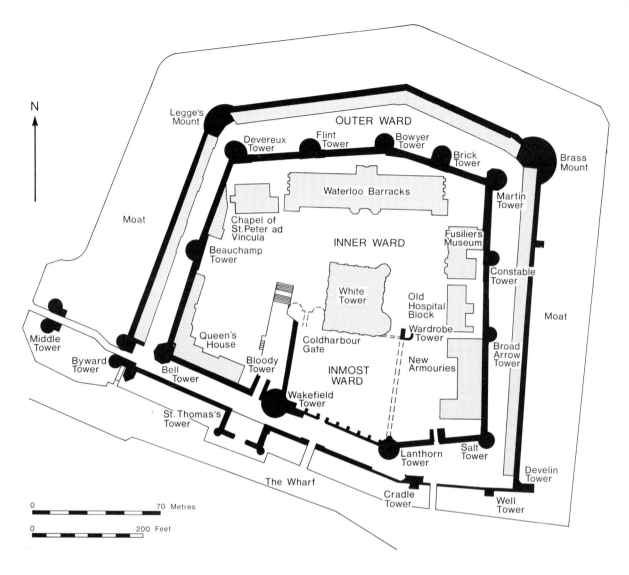

N

OUTER WARD

Legge's
Mount

Devereux
Tower

Flint
Tower

Bowyer
Tower

Brick
Tower

Brass
Mount

Moat

Waterloo Barracks

Martin
Tower

Chapel of
St.Peter ad
Vincula

INNER WARD

Fusiliers
Museum

Beauchamp
Tower

Constable
Tower

White
Tower

Old
Hospital
Block

Middle
Tower

Queen's
House

Coldharbour
Gate

Wardrobe
Tower

Broad
Arrow
Tower

Moat

Byward
Tower

Bloody
Tower

**INMOST
WARD**

New
Armouries

Bell
Tower

Wakefield
Tower

St. Thomas's
Tower

Lanthorn
Tower

Salt
Tower

Develin
Tower

The Wharf

Cradle
Tower

Well
Tower

0   70 Metres

0   200 Feet

1 *General plan of the Tower showing the three
wards of the castle and the principal buildings*
(English Heritage).

10

Introduction

The Tower of London has for centuries been at the heart of English history and is so closely associated with famous personalities and the images they have come to represent that its complex building story has all too often been overlooked or misunderstood. The castle is one of the most written about buildings in the world, but many authors have gone for the Crown Jewels or, more frequently, the state prisoners, helping to weave what the late Professor Allen Brown described as the 'morbid myth of a grim fortress-prison'. But the Tower was always much more a collection of self-contained communities whose activities were largely unaffected by the sombre business of detention. Besides being a royal residence, it was for hundreds of years the home of the Zoo, the Record Office, the Board of Ordnance and the Royal Mint. These bodies constantly sought to renew and improve their facilities and in so doing produced what can probably be described as the most redeveloped site in the country.

The greater part of the Tower's history falls within the period that followed the Middle Ages and during this time the building activities of the various departments were intense. Some of this work has previously only been loosely sketched out, while more has not been described at all. Most of the buildings dating from c.1500–1850 have now gone, but a wealth of documentary evidence, for instance in the form of building accounts, correspondence and drawings, remains to illustrate a good deal about their design, position and function.

The earlier history of the Tower as a royal fortress and residence relies more heavily on archaeological evidence, much of which has only come to light during the past thirty years. Important discoveries have been made regarding the development of the site in the Roman period, together with tantalizing indications of a late Saxon presence. Ditches associated with the formation of the early Norman fortress have been found and the subsequent expansion of the defences during the late twelfth and thirteenth centuries has largely been unravelled.

Topographically the 7 ha (18 acres) of the Tower divide into three fortified wards (encompassing just over 5 ha (12 acres), the Wharf and the outlying Liberties – a strip of ground beyond the moat which for reasons of military security was jealously guarded. The innermost, or Inmost Ward, comprises the central and earliest part of the castle, laid out during the Norman period within the angle of the surviving Roman city walls. To the north, east and west, this is surrounded by the Inner Ward, an area partly added during the reign of Richard I, the remainder during that of Henry III. Beyond lies the Outer Ward, the fortified corridor created by Edward I at the end of the thirteenth century and defining the castle's ultimate expansion. Needless to say, any description of the Tower is structured around these delineated areas.

1
Before the Normans

During the prehistoric and early Roman periods the southern margins of the site of the future Tower of London formed an area periodically flooded by the river Thames. Excavations within the south-east corner of the Inmost Ward in 1955 and 1976 revealed a noticeable bend in the clay bank of the river beneath accumulated water-lain silts. From the tops of these silts were recovered worn sherds of prehistoric pottery and flint flakes, representing the earliest indications discovered for human activity in the locality.

Towards the end of the prehistoric era the river levels receded leaving the area dry. That there was some occupation along the river

2 *Iron Age burial discovered to the north-west of the Lanthorn Tower during excavations in 1976* (photo: Derek Craig).

bank has been shown by discoveries that include a large pit containing Iron Age pottery, and at least one burial – a shallow grave containing the skeleton of a young male (**2**). The latter has been dated by radiocarbon analysis to the immediate pre-Roman period. Despite these finds, it is not thought that London at this time was the site of a substantial settlement.

The early Roman occupation
The Roman invasion of AD 43 and the foundation of *Londinium* did not immediately affect the area now occupied by the Tower. The area of major development was round the river Walbrook some 800m (2625 ft) to the west. The gradual spread of the city saw the marshy riverside area of the Inmost Ward reclaimed by the end of the first century AD and during the

following century two successive timber-framed buildings, probably houses, were constructed on the site. This development might have been linked to the construction nearby of a substantial masonry building. Its partial examination in 1956 indicated that most of it stood on the ground now occupied by the White Tower (3). Further masonry walls located near the opposing south-west corner of the keep, including a hypocaust found in 1899 and a buttressed wall excavated in 1975, may be related. It is probable that these remains represent ribbon development along the Roman road through the area, the line of which is preserved in Great Tower Street. The importance of this road is suggested by the fact that its line served as the earliest entraces to the Tower of London (see below, p. 17)

The building of the city defences

Around 200 the landward side of the city was surrounded by an impressive defensive wall just over 3km (2 miles) long. The south-east portion of this wall was of crucial importance to the future layout of the Tower, for it was this which was to form the eastern limit of the castle for nearly two hundred years. A small section of the Roman wall can still be seen behind the remains of the Wardrobe Tower, near the south-east corner of the White Tower. The masonry is nearly 2.4m (8 ft) wide above a projecting sandstone plinth; the external faces, here as elsewhere, are composed of neat rows of squared ragstone with tile bonding courses set at regular intervals. Excavation has shown that just north of where it is exposed there is a slight change in alignment, and at this point there was a small internal turret (see 3), which in addition to providing access on to the wall would have acted as a look-out.

During construction of this section of the wall and its wide internal earth rampart, it is known that much of the masonry building that occupied the site was left standing. This provides a sharp contrast to the situation further down the hill where the latest of the timber-framed buildings previously mentioned was demolished to make way for the defences. The building occupying the site of the White Tower may, therefore, have been particularly important or significant.

Of equal importance to the early history of the Tower was the subsequent development of the riverside defences. Recent investigations have shown that these were added in the second half of the third century and can be seen as a direct response to the threat of a sea-borne attack. A section of the wall revealed in 1977 below Water Lane to the west of the Lanthorn Tower was found to be supported by a mass of substantial oak piles. The growth rings of these piles were cross matched with timbers recovered from beneath other parts of the river wall and have been dated 255–70. Historically this was a period of grave trouble, for Britain was part of the breakaway Gallic Empire which separated from the control of the Roman authorities for a period of 14 years following the usurpation of Postumus in 259. It was during this independence that the threat of Saxon sea-borne incursions first became acute and a number of the 'Saxon Shore' forts around the coast of southern England are thought to have been built in the 270s and 280s.

The late remodelling of the city defences

During the final years of the fourth century a remarkable remodelling of the river defences took place in the extreme south-east corner of the city. A meticulously constructed wall 3.2m (10 ft 6 in) wide was built 4m (13 ft) to the north of the earlier one on the same east-west alignment (4). Some 14.5m (47 ft) west of the landward wall it turned south at an angle of 105° to connect with the earlier river wall; a possible gate or postern was formed at this point providing access down on to the foreshore or wharf. The overall effect was to create a promontory at the corner of the defences guarding the river approach to the city (see 3). During excavations in 1976–7 and 1979 numerous late fourth-century coins were found in deposits below and against the wall which securely date its construction to a period after 388. As such, the wall not only represents the latest Roman defence so far identified in London, but also the latest Roman military work yet found in Britain.

The remodelling of the city's eastern river defence may not have been carried out in isolation, for late Roman alterations to London's walls have been recorded elsewhere. These include repairs to the river wall at Blackfriars, at the eastern end of the waterfront, and the addition of bastions at regular intervals to the eastern half of the landward wall. At the same time the digging of a new, wide, flat-bottomed ditch provided an unrestricted field of

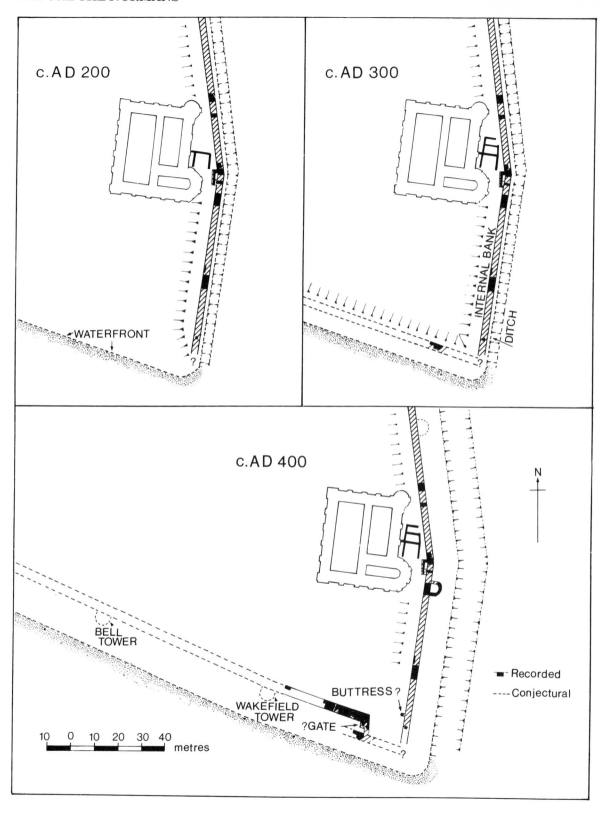

c.AD 200

WATERFRONT

c.AD 300

INTERNAL BANK

DITCH

c.AD 400

N

BELL
TOWER

BUTTRESS?

WAKEFIELD
TOWER

?GATE

■ Recorded
---- Conjectural

10 0 10 20 30 40
metres

4 *Section of the late fourth-century Roman riverside wall uncovered between the Lanthorn and Wakefield towers during excavations in 1976* (photo: Jeremy Hall, Royal Armouries).

fire for spring guns which may have been mounted on top of the towers. The remains of one of these bastions was incorporated into the twelfth-century Wardrobe Tower near the south-east corner of the White Tower.

The river wall also might have been furnished with bastions and it has been argued that the Lanthorn, Wakefield and Bell towers, along the southern inner curtain wall, could have originated as Roman mural towers since the distances between them are similar to those recorded between Roman bastions on the landward wall.

3 *Development of the south-east corner of the Roman city defences circa* AD *200–400 in relationship to the site of White Tower* (Author).

The alterations to the river defences at the Tower are not the only evidence for late Roman activity in the extreme south-east corner of the city. New floors, including a tessellated pavement, were laid in the middle of the fourth century in part of the building revealed to the east of the White Tower, with occupation certainly continuing for some time after that. To the north-east of the Wakefield Tower excavation has revealed the remains of a mortared floor which post-dates the rebuilding of the river wall, and thus quite probably dates to the early years of the fifth century. Furthermore, a stamped silver ingot together with gold coins of Arcadius and Honorius, also probably dating to the early fifth century, were found in 1777 while digging foundation trenches near the Lanthorn Tower. During the late Roman period officially stamped ingots of this type were probably used to pay soldiers and officials: a late Roman document attests the presence of a Treasury in London. At least one, and probably three, additional ingots were found on Tower Hill in 1898, providing further evidence for an official presence in this part of the city. These hoards, the remodelling of the defences and the evidence for building work within the walls, may support the old tradition, sceptically rehearsed by John Stow in the sixteenth century, that the Tower originated as a Roman stronghold.

After the Romans

At present little archaeological evidence for the history of the site between the beginning of the fifth century and the construction of William the Conqueror's fortress in 1067 is available. Such evidence as there is appears to relate to the very end of the Saxon period. Some idea of what happened to Roman life-styles at this period can, however, be gleaned from excavations to the west of the castle at Billingsgate. Here a late Roman house with private bath-house was found to have been abandoned about the end of the first quarter of the fifth century. Thereafter debris accumulated over the floors before decay caused a tiled roof to collapse leaving the building roofless and at the mercy of the elements. Nearby, the riverfront lay abandoned, with wharfs slowly being covered by silts washed down from the hillside.

Archaeological evidence for decay and abandonment within the Roman city is relatively plentiful, but the signs of Saxon occupation of the fifth to seventh centuries are not. In the last few years, however, investigations have thrown considerable light on this enigma, with the discovery of the site of a major Saxon settlement to the west of the present-day City of London, along the Strand. There is no doubt that this was in existence by the end of the seventh century and that it grew in size and importance during the eighth and into the ninth century. By the end of the ninth century, with the threat of Viking raids, the town appears to have begun to relocate within the old walled city.

An ecclesiastical presence had already been re-established there much earlier, beginning with the foundation of St Paul's Cathedral in 604. The earliest surviving remains of a church, however, are those found in All Hallows, Barking, on Tower Hill immediately outside the Tower, where bombing during the Second World War revealed a Saxon doorway which may date from the eighth century.

As far as the Tower itself is concerned, the only tantalizing evidence of pre-Norman occupation comes from excavations carried out in advance of the construction of the present Jewel Chamber. Here, a large ditch running north-west to south-east, much cut about by later work, was discovered. Engineers' drawings prepared in 1845 and showing the foundations of the Waterloo Barracks immediately to the north of these excavations, confirm the presence of a wide ditch up to 5m (16 ft) in depth, on approximately the same line. What little pottery was recovered from the fill of the ditch can only be described as Anglo-Norman in character. This ditch may have surrounded an enclosure of late Saxon date, but until more of it is discovered, no conclusions can be reached about the exact date and nature of the earthworks.

2

The Norman castle

After William the Conqueror's triumphant coronation in Westminster Abbey on Christmas Day 1066, his biographer, William of Poitiers, states that the king withdrew to Barking in Essex 'while certain strongholds were made in the city against the fickleness of the vast and fierce population'. Writing some hundred years later William Fitzstephen mentions two strongly fortified castles to the west. These can be identified as Baynard's Castle and Montfichet's Tower, both located to the south-west of St Paul's Cathedral. The Norman Baynard's Castle was slighted during the reign of King John, while Montfichet's Tower was evidently in ruins by the end of the twelfth century; both sites were transferred to the Blackfriars in 1275 and whatever survived of the fortifications presumably disappeared as the Dominicans set about constructing their friary.

The earliest defences
In the east of the City another of the Conqueror's castles was the future Tower of London which was set in the south-east angle of the Roman defences. Some writers have suggested that a second fortification existed here too, either as an adjunct to the castle, or as part of a pre-White Tower structure set within it. This theory is based on a reference in a charter of 1141 between the Empress Maud and Geoffrey de Mandeville, granting him custody of 'the tower of London with the little castle which was Ravenger's'. Of Ravenger nothing is known save that he was a Norman landholder who was apparently dead by the time of Domesday Survey. The enigmatic terminology of the grant is replaced by the more normal wording of 'the Tower of London with the castle which is beneath it' in a second charter by Maud, and in

another of Stephen's in the same year. This would seem to emphasize the distinction between keep and bailey. Ravenger may have been an early constable whose name was still associated with the castle in the middle of the twelfth century.

What then is known about the form of the early enclosure? Much remains obscure, but excavations have revealed two early ditches to the north and south-west of the White Tower (**5**). The ditches were directed to points along the Roman city walls where the regular spacing would anticipate bastions. The ditch north of the White Tower, some 8m (25 ft) wide and 3.5m (11 ft) deep, was located running north-east to south-west, cutting through the late Saxon ditch and turning south from a point near the north-west corner of the White Tower. The second ditch, which had a similar V-shaped profile, was located running north from the Wakefield Tower (**6**). A simple projection of the two does not produce a straight line. However, the presence of Roman remains near the south-east corner of the White Tower may have influenced the layout; indeed a substantial Roman wall was found jutting into the ditch just south of the Coldharbour Gate. These anomalies could be explained if the original gate into the enclosure lay at this point and utilized part of the Roman building as a footing or abutment. It should be recalled that a gate in this position would represent the forerunner of the thirteenth-century Coldharbour Gate, which straddled the road of known Roman origin, the line of which is today taken by Great Tower Street.

The Conqueror's enclosure, bounded by Roman walls to the south and east and ditches to the north and west, doubtless reinforced

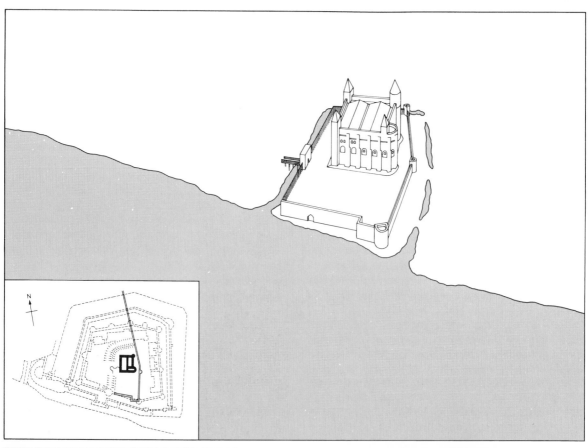

with earth ramparts and wooden palisades, occupied an area of some 0.5ha (1¼ acres). Compared to other early Norman castles this appears small, though there are examples elsewhere of castles which occupied 0.4ha (1 acre) or less, including Totnes, Shrewsbury and Wigmore. Nevertheless, it might have been supposed that William's principal London fortress would have been larger, rather than smaller, than average. Not surprisingly this has led to suggestions that an outer bailey may have existed to the west though at present the only evidence for this is circumstantial (see below).

The White Tower

As for the date when work began on the White Tower, the great stone keep which was to give the castle its popular name, we know only for certain that it was being constructed in the last decade of William's reign (1066–87). The register of the cathedral priory of Rochester, *Textus Roffensis*, describes how a certain piece of London property came into the possession of the monks there, at the time when Gundulf, Bishop of Rochester, was 'in charge of the work of the great tower of London'. The same document describes how the bishop subsequently came to build Rochester Castle for William II, and adds that he was 'very competent and skilful at building in stone'. Gundulf's supervision of the building of the White Tower presumably began after 1077, the year in which he was appointed to his see. Work was likely to have been finished before 1100 when it was reported that Ranulf Flambard, Bishop of Durham, was imprisoned in the building.

Designed as a fortified palace, *Arx Palatina* as William Fitzstephen called it, the White Tower is still one of the potent symbols of Norman authority (**7**). To the native Saxon population of London, unfamiliar with build-

5 *The Tower in c.1100. On the small plan earlier buildings are tinted and new buildings shown solid (see also* **11**, **17** *and* **19***)* (English Heritage).

6 *Lower part of the Norman defensive ditch to the north of the Wakefield Tower as revealed by excavation in 1975. The footings on the right belong to Henry III's western inner curtain wall* (photo: Derek Craig).

7 *The White Tower viewed from the south-west showing the reconstructed entrance stairs* (photo: Jeremy Hall, Royal Armouries).

ings of such scale and appearance, it must have provided a vivid reminder that a new order had been established. Measuring 35m (118 ft) by 29m (97 ft), excluding the apse and turret projections, and rising on the south side to a height of 27m (90 ft) to its battlements, it was only exceeded in size by the contemporary, but less complex castle at Colchester (**8**). No obvious models for these two buildings are known, but it has been suggested that they may have been influenced to some extent by the great tenth-century tower within the castle of Rouen in Normandy which was demolished in 1204. Their design, however, may owe as much to local conditions and initiatives – at Colchester by the layout of the Roman temple which the Norman castle was built over and at the Tower by the need to provide large-scale accommodation within the constraints of a relatively small enclosure.

LONDON
THE WHITE TOWER

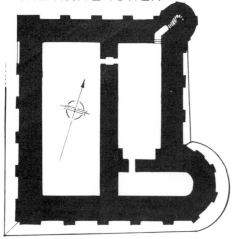

COLCHESTER
THE TOWER

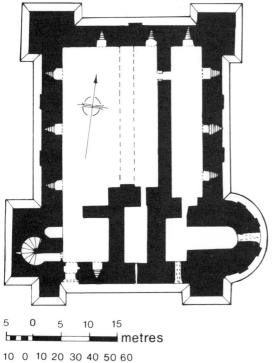

5 0   5   10   15
metres

10 0 10 20 30 40 50 60
Scale in feet

8 *Comparative floor plans of the White Tower and the keep at Colchester Castle* (English Heritage).

Investigations have shown that the apse on the south-east corner of the White Tower was added after the basement walls were constructed. This discovery has led to the suggestion that the idea came from Colchester where the apse was derived from the underlying Roman structure. Apart from this detail, the plan of the White Tower appears to have been settled at an early date. The principal building stone is Kentish ragstone with some Septana – a mud-stone from the Thames – found in the plinth. Caen stone from Normandy, supplemented with some Quarr stone from the royal quarries on the Isle of Wight, provides the architectural enrichments and ashlar, though little now survives on the exterior as this was largely replaced by Portland stone in the seventeeth and eighteenth centuries.

Internally the building originally comprised two storeys above a basement (**9**). The basement was for storage and could only be reached by the main staircase in the north-east turret. It is partly terraced into the hillside so that much of the northern half lies below ground level. As with the floors above, it is divided into three compartments, of which the principal, western, room contains the well. The interiors, however, owe much of their present appearance to the eighteenth century when the floor levels were lowered and the existing large brick valuts constructed to replace an earlier timber arrangement (**colour plate 9**).

The entrance floor above, probably intended for the use of the constable and other important officials, could only be entered by a doorway in the south wall. This was re-opened in 1973 after three hundred years of redundancy and a timber staircase built to suggest something of the original approach (see **7**). Of the two great rooms on the ground floor, which must have been subdivided to some extent by wooden partitions, that to the east must have been the more important, since it controls access to the royal suite above. It also covers entry into the chapel crypt, which has a small square chamber formed within the thickness of the north wall. The windowless form and restricted access, suggest that it was designed as a strong-room for the safekeeping of royal treasures and important documents.

The principal floor of the White Tower was the upper floor, comprising a grand residential suite of hall (to the west), chamber and chapel.

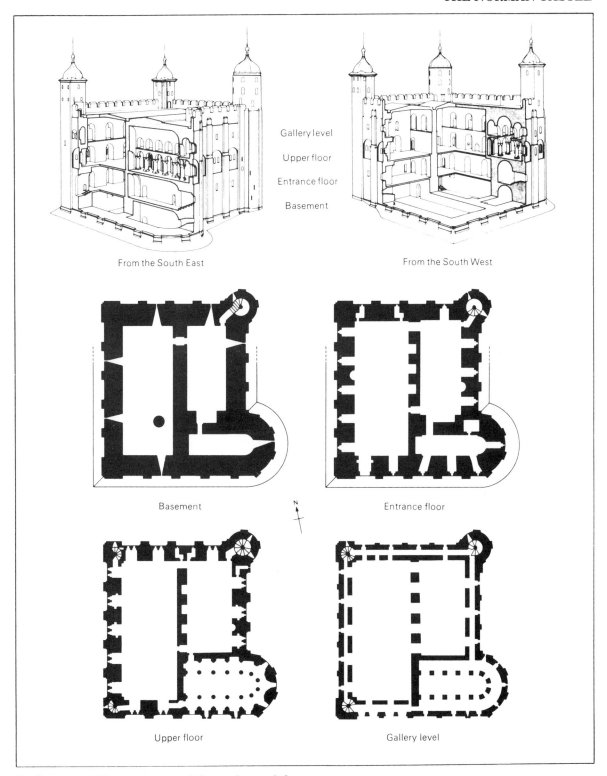

Gallery level

Upper floor

Entrance floor

Basement

From the South East

From the South West

Basement

Entrance floor

Upper floor

Gallery level

9 *Cut-away illustrations and floor plans of the White Tower* (English Heritage).

10 *The south aisle of the Chapel of St John in the White Tower showing details of columns and vault* (Historic Royal Palaces Agency).

Finally, there is the Chapel of St John. Though devoid of any colour, which must have decorated its walls and columns, the chapel now stands as the best preserved interior within the building. Its architecture is plain and bold and presents an important record of the Anglo-Norman Romanesque influences at work at the time of the invasion (**10**). Here, more than anywhere else, the visitor can experience something of the environment that the first Norman monarch of England sought to create for himself.

The later Norman period
By the end of the eleventh century the first phase of the building history of the Tower seems to have been complete, with the great tower and its bailey surrounded by the Roman city walls to the south and east, and defensive ditches to the north and west. The Roman walls would have been in need of repair and some scant evidence for this has been observed along the riverside wall, including a fragment of Norman style herring-bone masonry on the re-entrant to the west of the Lanthorn Tower, suggesting perhaps that the postulated Roman postern at this point continued in use.

Little is known about the building history of the Tower after c.1100 and before the works carried out during the reign of Richard I at the end of the twelfth century. The *Anglo-Saxon Chronicle* records that William Rufus caused a wall to be built about the Tower in 1097, presumably to replace the Conqueror's earthen ramparts and wooden palisades. During the reign of Henry II the 'King's apartments in the bailey' are known to have been repaired in 1171–2, thus demonstrating that before this date the royal lodgings had grown beyond the limits of the White Tower. Doubtless structures occupied the bailey from the earliest period and excavations at other Norman castles, such as Hen Domen and Launceston, have revealed baileys crowded with buildings during the eleventh- and early twelfth-century periods. Excavations along the south side of the Inmost Ward have shown that at an early date the ground level behind the Roman riverside wall was substantially lowered, but only for a short period of time before being raised again. No evidence for any building activity was recorded and the purpose of this temporary scarping of the bailey is difficult to determine.

To the reign of Henry II (1154–89) may be

The hall and chamber originally rose two full stages to the underside of the roof, with a mural gallery encircling the outer walls at the level of the present, inserted, floor. The chamber, like the two main rooms on the floor below, boasts an original fireplace in the east wall; together these represent the earliest features of their kind to be found anywhere in the country. There is no evidence for a fireplace in the hall, so it must be assumed that the room was heated by a brazier with smoke escaping through louvres in the roof. The south wall of the hall, at gallery level, still contains, albeit restored, four original two-light windows. Elsewhere in the building all the windows were enlarged in the eighteenth century.

attributed the forebuilding, a large, square, masonry tower, added to protect the entrance to the White Tower. Although only a few offsets, cut into the plinth on the south face of the keep, now mark the site of the structure, it can clearly be identified on the late Elizabethan survey (see **36**). Also to the twelfth century may be assigned the surviving medieval remains of the Wardrobe Tower, built directly on to the base of a late Roman bastion and evidently linked to the south-east corner of the White Tower with a contemporary pilaster buttressed wall that was demolished in 1883 (see **76**).

3

The Tower enlarged

When the second Plantagenet king, Richard I, came to the throne in 1189 he almost immediately departed to the Holy Land leaving his chancellor, William Longchamp, to administer the realm. This proved to be the beginning of a period of great importance for the Tower, as

11 *The Tower in c.1200* (English Heritage).

Longchamp at once began to improve its fortifications.

The Pipe Roll of 1190 shows that the constable of the Tower was allowed an expenditure of no less than £2881 for the 49 weeks ending on 11 November. The principal development described by the contemporary chronicler, Roger of Howden, records how Longchamp,

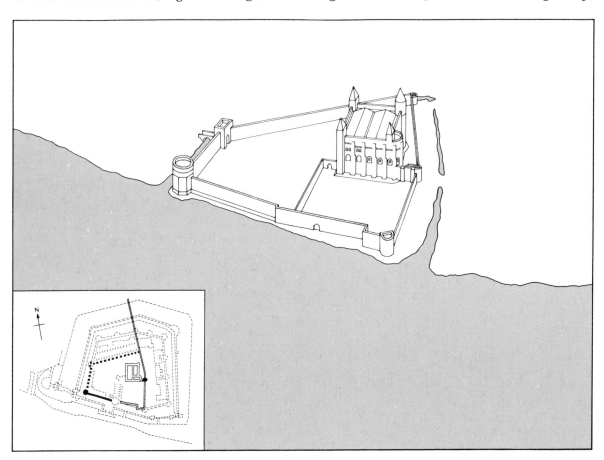

immediately upon his arrival, had a deep ditch dug round the Tower 'hoping that the water from the Thames would flow through it'. A second commentator, Matthew Paris, adds that the attempt failed, presumably because of inadequate sluicing arrangements to retain the Thames water at low tide. The ditch referred to was almost certainly a massive feature discovered in advance of the construction of the Jewel House in 1963–4. On the same north-east to south-west alignment as the earlier Norman ditch, which it almost obliterated (see above, p. 17), the new ditch was cut to a depth of some 6m (19 ft) and was directed towards the Beauchamp Tower, from where it presumably turned south to meet the Thames (**11**).

Work on the Tower was still in progress when the king's brother, John, entered London on the night of 7/8 October 1191 and rallied an alliance of barons and Londoners to challenge Longchamp's authority. The unpopular bishop took refuge in the Tower, but although the incomplete walls held, he lacked sufficient provisions for siege and was obliged to surrender.

The Bell Tower

The only surviving masonry associated with this phase is the Bell Tower and the lower half of the adjoining curtain to the east (**12**). They are assumed to occupy the line of the Roman river wall and it has been suggested that the Bell Tower was built on the remains of a bastion. In order to withstand the action of the Thames which washed their bases, both tower and wall are constructed on a substantial plinth of seven offsets of Sussex marble. The original facing above this, where it still survives, is composed of Reigate sandstone. A great deal of the same material can be found within the well-preserved interiors, particularly on the ground floor which features a fine vault with plain square ribs springing from moulded corbels. This is the earliest known use in the castle of Reigate stone, which continued to be widely employed until the sixteenth century.

The form of the Bell Tower is unusual in so far as it is octagonal in shape up to the top of the ground floor, but thereafter cylindrical. This awkward change might be explained if the tower was built in two stages. Polygonal and circular forms in mural towers and keeps are fairly common in the late twelfth century. They were developed to provide greater protection

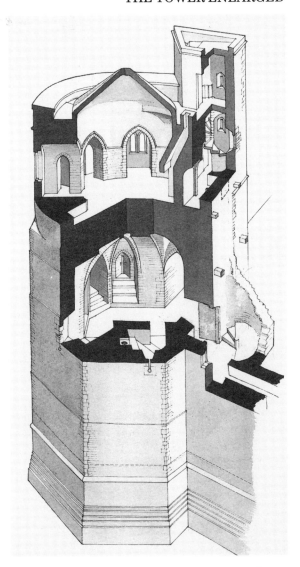

12 *Cut-away illustration of the Bell Tower showing the upper and lower chambers and the suggested arrangement of the adjoining stair turret and mural passage* (Terry Ball).

against attackers trying to undermine or batter the bases of towers. Furthermore, whereas the flat surfaces of earlier rectangular towers took the full impact of missiles, faceted or curved walls could deflect them. The polygonal form of the Bell Tower may be compared, for example, with the Avranches Tower at Dover and the Butavent Tower at Corfe. Both are royal works located at critical angles of the defences, and both date to this period.

The lower part of the Bell Tower forms a solid base no less than 5.5m (18 ft) in depth. One reason for this might be if the structure engulfed the remains of a Roman river bastion; but excavations in 1958 in the Boiler Room of the Queen's House immediately north of the Bell Tower suggest a quite different explanation. Here the construction trench for the thirteenth-century west curtain wall was found to have cut through a considerable depth of clay. Bore-hole surveys on Tower Green immediately to the east indicate that the top of natural London Clay is there reached about 4m (13 ft) lower. This localized build-up of clay may be part of a bank aligned north–south, and perhaps associated with a ditch. The bank, if it is indeed one, pre-dates Edward I's curtain wall of the 1270s and could be associated with Longchamp's works of the 1190s, so accounting for the ground floor of the Bell Tower being constructed at such a high level. Alternatively, this possible bank might be earlier and perhaps provides evidence for an early outer bailey to the castle.

In the medieval castle, mural towers invariably performed two functions: firstly, they provided covering fire along adjoining curtain walls and into the dead zones in front of neighbouring towers; and, secondly, they provided domestic accommodation. In the late eleventh or twelfth centuries, mural towers were normally rectangular and often open-backed with timber framing forming rear walls, as at Framlingham and Arundel. More often than not, ground floors were poorly lit and would not have been intended for lodgings. Even the upper floors were usually entered from the wall walks, with walkways traversing them, and would have afforded rather spartan accommodation with neither fireplace nor garderobe. From the middle of the twelfth century mural towers proliferated and at the same time both their defensive and domestic arrangements greatly improved.

Thus the Bell Tower, the only complete mural tower from the time of Richard I to survive at the Tower, was provided with spacious accommodation on both the ground and upper floors, each equipped with a garderobe. The upper chamber, not surprisingly is the grander, it is furnished with a fireplace and incorporates a mural passage in the west wall. Investigations during the 1970s revealed the remains of a stair turret attached to the east side of the tower, which originally connected ground and upper floors, and also a length of mural passage partly contrived within the thickness of the adjoining south curtain wall. It is probable that both went out of use before the rebuilding of the Queen's House in 1540, perhaps as early as the mid-fourteenth century when the constable's lodgings were reconstructed (see below, p. 49).

4

The classic castle

When Henry III came to the throne in 1216, the Tower, like most of the castles in the south-east of England, had yielded to the French dauphin, Louis VIII, whose invading armies had advanced as far as Wiltshire in the west and Leicestershire in the north. Henry, hurriedly and rather unceremoniously crowned at Gloucester, was almost a refugee in his own land. However, several major fortresses, including Dover and Windsor, stubbornly resisted the French onslaught, loyalist supporters rallied, and after a decisive land battle at Lincoln in May 1217 and the sea battle off Dover in August 1217 the Angevin dynasty was saved. The advisers to the young king saw the immediate repair and modernization of the royal castles as an essential part of the re-establishment of the Crown's authority. Though, as discussed above, considerable sums had been spent on the Tower during the reign of Richard I, it seems clear that the castle's defences were considered inadequate.

During Henry's long reign (1216–72) hardly a year went by when work of one sort or another was not in progress at the Tower; the total expenditure, during and after the king's minority (which ended in 1227), amounted to nearly £10,000. Only the great works at Windsor castle exceeded this, at a cost of £15,000. The general scope of these building operations is well understood, even though the sequence and degree of completeness is not always clear.

The minority of Henry III and the rebuilding of the Palace Ward

The major building works during the 1220s and 1230s were concentrated on the inner bailey, that is to say the Inmost Ward, where the existing royal lodgings were refurbished and enlarged to provide a degree of residential splendour worthy of comparison with any of those created for the King at Windsor, Clarendon or Winchester. Work effectively began in about 1220 with the construction of two towers, the larger being the Wakefield Tower, the other, apparently far enough advanced to be roofed in lead in 1225–6, probably being the Lanthorn Tower. In contemporary accounts the Wakefield Tower is referred to either as the Blundeville Tower, after the then constable of the Tower, John de Blundeville, or the Hall Tower, owing to its proximity to the great hall in the bailey. The Lanthorn Tower was demolished in 1776 after being gutted by fire, but its plan is recorded in detailed eighteenth-century surveys. The Wakefield Tower still stands and together with its environs has been the subject of considerable archaeological work.

Both towers occupied the suggested sites of Roman bastions, whose regular spacing appears to have determined the dimensions of the Inmost Ward, and both were constructed with adjoining chamber blocks overlooking the river (**colour plate 1**). Excavations have shown that the plan of the chamber attached to the west side of the Lanthorn Tower was partly determined by the Roman riverside defences, the south and west walls representing a substantial rebuilding of the re-entrant in the line of the river wall.

Where the north wall of the chamber block joined the Lanthorn Tower, a spiral staircase was contrived in the thickness of the masonry to provide access to the royal apartments above. The Lanthorn Tower was unusual among the mural towers of Henry III for having three, as opposed to two, floors. In fact it is worth noting that the only other example with

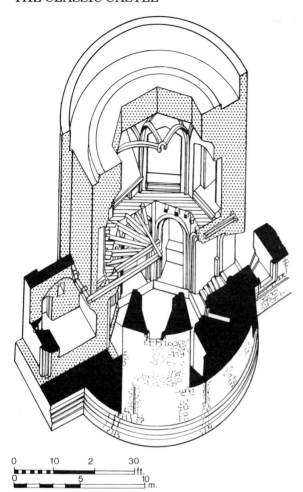

0 10 2 30 ft.
0 5 10 m.

13 *Cut-away illustration of the Wakefield Tower showing the original timberwork of the ground-floor ceiling* (English Heritage).

three floors was the Salt Tower which, erected some twenty years later, also occupies a strategic point on the corner of the defences overlooking the Thames.

Turning to the Wakefield Tower, excavations in 1957 revealed the lower south face of the adjoining chamber block, which incorporated the remains of a private water-gate hard against the tower (**13**). The cill of the gate is pierced with weep-holes to allow any water which penetrated the passage to escape. The gate led directly into the ground floor of the tower and/or up a spacious spiral staircase 3m (10 ft) in diameter to the state apartments above. In front of the postern the remains of a timber landing stage were found (**colour plate 2**).

Some 10m (33 ft) east of the Wakefield Tower the base of the chamber block abutted against an earlier structure comprised of two north-south walls set 2.4m (8 ft) apart. Between them the main drain of the palace discharged in a fine barrel-vaulted culvert which, when discovered in 1899, was found to extend as far north as the south-west turret of the White Tower (**14**). The footings of the flanking walls were observed to extend some way south of the upstanding masonry. They had, therefore, been cut back at some stage to resemble buttresses. The purpose of this structure can only be guessed, but it might have appeared as a small rectangular tower or some sort of open-fronted barbican or water-gate projecting towards the river.

There can be no doubt that of the two suites created by Henry in the Inmost Ward, that incorporating the Wakefield Tower was the grandest and intended for his own use. It can be reasonably assumed that the other was for his queen. Located either side of the great hall this arrangement represents an interesting, and early, formation of a king's and queen's side in royal planning. A fortified pentice occupying the line of the Roman riverside wall evidently provided access between the two suites (**colour plate 1**). Here, as with Henry's royal lodgings at Westminster, Clarendon, Clipstone and elsewhere, the principal rooms were located on the first floor. The chambers within the Lanthorn and Wakefield towers would have been the most prestigious, being the king's and queen's innermost sanctums where they would have retired for rest or private conversation. Here also would have been found the monarch's bed, the principal piece of furniture – a simple canopied device covered with hangings. For Henry III's period we have for the first time a clear idea of how the royal lodgings were decorated. In 1238 the walls of the queen's chamber were ordered to be whitewashed and painted with false pointing (to imitate stone) and flowers. Only two years later it was to be wainscoted, whitewashed and painted with roses, while a panelled partition wall was to be erected between the chamber and garderobe and a tiled floor laid. At the same time the king's great chamber (presumably in the Wakefield Tower) was redecorated and, in an age which knew no curtains, provided with window shutters painted with the royal arms.

The building of the Wakefield Tower was

14 *The main drain of Henry III's palace show-ing an addition of Edward I's reign (nearest to the camera) which extended the tunnel south-wards and thus allowed it to discharge through the new river curtain. Throughout much of its length the drain is some 2m (6 ft) in depth (Historic Royal Palaces Agency).*

carried out in conjunction with the eastward continuation of Longchamp's river curtain and the provision of a new wall and gate-tower to defend the western side of the Inmost Ward. It is clear from investigations that this did not represent a single programme of work, but several, carried out over a period of between 15 and 20 years (**15**).

Excavations carried out in Water Lane have revealed the eastern limit of Longchamp's cur-tain wall (that is to say the point where it reached the outer edge of the Norman ditch), immediately below the western jamb of the Bloody Tower. Grafted on to this wall were the lower courses of Henry's wall, faced in Reigate sandstone (as opposed to Longchamp's Sussex marble) and given a plinth of three offsets to withstand the tidal action of the Thames. The Bloody Tower gateway above is of the same build as Henry's curtain wall with the original roadway lying some 75cm (30 in) below the present cobbles. Although intended as the cas-tle's main water-gate the structure at first was of only modest strength and was defended by a portcullis and gate. A small guard-room stands to the east; it is integral with the construction of the gate and the Wakefield Tower and was originally entered from the north where the remains of a doorway can still be seen (see **13**).

To the north of the Wakefield Tower excava-tions showed that the Norman ditch had been infilled during the early stages of the building operation. This does not mean that the Inmost Ward was left undefended, for there can be no

29

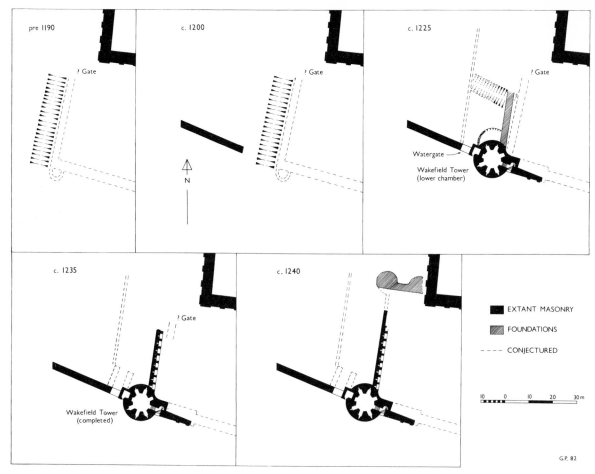

15 *Plan showing the development of the Wakefield Tower and its surroundings* (Author).

doubt that a stone wall was already in existence on the east side of the ditch at a much earlier date; it was probably this wall that accounted for the north-south alignment of several large cess pits found dug into the fill of the ditch.

The same excavations revealed that the building of the Wakefield Tower and the curtain wall to the north was carried out in stages. The base of the tower was faced with fine ashlar and set within a quadrant ditch (**16**). The adjoining section of the curtain wall, although constructed of rubble, was well coursed and given a rendered finish. To the north, however, the wall foundations showed different techniques of construction and appearance as the builders grappled with the problem of preparing their footing in the fill of the Norman ditch which had not yet had time to consolidate.

With the lower part of the Wakefield Tower constructed and some 26m (84 ft) of foundations for the curtain wall to the north of it laid, the west side of the ditch around the base of the Wakefield Tower was then revetted with a rubble wall and the ditch infilled. Though well coursed and of stout build the revetment was not intended to be seen and must, therefore, have been constructed in the knowledge that the base of the Wakefield Tower was to be concealed. The east wall of the Bloody Tower relies on the revetment as a foundation and there seems little doubt that this is what it was intended for. Thus it can be supposed that at an early stage in the building operation it was decided to enlarge the water-gate into a gatehouse proper. A reference in 1225 to the 'small tower which the king has ordered to be built' may relate to this conversion. Perhaps as a precaution while work was in progress, or alternatively while matters were at a standstill, a temporary defensive ditch was excavated on

16 *The northern base of the Wakefield Tower during excavations in 1975. The lower part of the western inner curtain wall can be seen on the left* (photo: Jeremy Hall, Royal Armouries).

an east–west alignment to the north. It is assumed to have been only a short line of defence extending between the earlier wall of the Inmost Ward and another running north from the Bloody Tower (on the line of the present one) which retained the higher ground to the west. After a short period the ditch was infilled and work on the main body of the upstanding curtain wall with its formidable row of embrasures and loops began.

The final stage of work on the western defences of the Inmost Ward involved the completion of the curtain wall and the building of the Coldharbour Gate itself, the main entrance into the bailey near the south-east corner of the White Tower. The fact that this was treated as a separate parcel of work might suggest that there had been an intention, albeit as a temporary measure, to utilize the earlier entrance. In this respect the anomalous arrangement of wall foundations near the south-west corner of the White Tower might be explained if they include remnants of an earlier gate. As for the identifiable Henrican remains, these indicate a gate-house of typical thirteenth-century form comprising two cylindrical towers, either side of a gate-passage.

The completion of the western defences of the Inmost Ward must have been achieved by 1238 when Henry turned his attention to the enlargement of the castle. By this time many of the improvements to the palace were finished. These included the building of a new kitchen, probably to the east of the hall, in 1230, and the virtual reconstruction of the great hall during the early 1230s. The latter was presumably near completion in 1234 when the external walls were whitewashed. The hall was unusual in so far as its plan, which can be identified on various seventeenth- and eighteenth-century surveys, was approximately square. It was in fact some 21m (70 ft) square and no doubt aisled in a manner similar to Henry's magnificent hall at Winchester.

In 1234 a crenellated chamber was built in front of the Wakefield Tower (perhaps as a penthouse over the adjoining chamber block?) and a pentice erected 'before the chapel and chamber of St Thomas's' (wherever that was). Henry's concern for the White Tower was shown in 1240 when its walls were whitewashed (doubtless a practice from which it derives its name) while lead pipes were extended down to the ground so that the rain did not spoil the new finish (**colour plate 1**). A projecting timber gallery was constructed on the top of the south side of the White Tower so that the base of the wall could be defended more effectively. Within, the Chapel of St John was to be whitewashed throughout and three glass windows painted with depictions of the Virgin and Child, the Holy Trinity and St John the Evangelist. The cross and beam over the altar were to be painted in gold colours and two images of St Edward offering the ring to St John the Evangelist provided.

A saucery 'large and fair' was built between the great hall and the kitchen in 1241 while new privy chambers, presumably attached to the Wakefield and Lanthorn towers, were constructed for the king and queen in 1246–7. It is not possible to identify the positions of many of the palace buildings from contemporary or later sources and sadly no archaeological evidence for any of them has yet been found. In fact the only medieval masonry recorded behind the line of the river curtain during excavations in 1976 were the foundations of a substantial wall and buttress, thought to represent the west end of the twelfth-century hall, and lying some 3.6m (12 ft) to the east of Henry's hall.

Of the palatial accommodation that Henry provided for himself, only the Wakefield Tower now remains. A formidable and noble structure, the building exhibits the duality of military strength and residential splendour. Restorations in the early 1970s revealed the original ground floor, some 2.6m (8 ft 6 ins) below an existing brick floor. Most of the infill was of late thirteenth-century date. The lower

masonry, therefore, was protected at an early date, as its excellent condition so clearly demonstrates. Evidently the dumping was intended to obviate flooding, after the construction of the outer curtain wall in the reign of Edward I impeded drainage of water into the Thames from the higher ground to the north. Investigations also disclosed evidence for the form of the original ceiling, thus confirming the accuracy of a drawing made by the architectural historian G.T. Clark shortly before the timberwork was replaced by a brick vault in 1867. The present reconstruction follows exactly the ingenious pattern of the original (see **13**); it should be noted, however, that the thirteenth-century joists were anchored into a ring beam set well within the walls of the tower. This, having rotted over the centuries, could not be replaced so in consequence a central post had to be installed to provide support.

The upper chamber, like the lower, has an octagonal plan with lofty recesses in each face. The partly mutilated north-east recess probably contained the garderobe while the south-east recess contained an oratory with aumbry, piscina and sedilia; in 1238 a screen was provided to divide it from the main chamber. When G.T. Clark visited the room shortly before its 'restoration' in 1867–9, he saw traces of a fresco on the walls of the oratory. Sadly by 1885 the artist H.W. Brewer was lamenting that no trace of it could be found. Brewer described the mural as depicting two figures; perhaps these were representations of Dives and Lazarus, a parable Henry had a strong liking for and which he had painted in the hall at Ludgershall in 1246 and on a glass window in the hall at Guildford in 1253.

The defences extended

In or about 1238 another and even more important series of works began which, with various delays and set-backs, was to continue throughout the rest of Henry III's reign. This involved the construction of a new towered curtain wall to the east of the old Roman landward wall and beyond Longchamp's ditch north of the White Tower. The ditch, together with its curtain wall, disappeared once the new defences were up (**17**). A Flemish expert, a certain Master John le Fosser, was engaged to ensure that the problem of retaining Thames water in the ditch, as experienced by Longchamp fifty years earlier, was not repeated. Beyond the ditch the

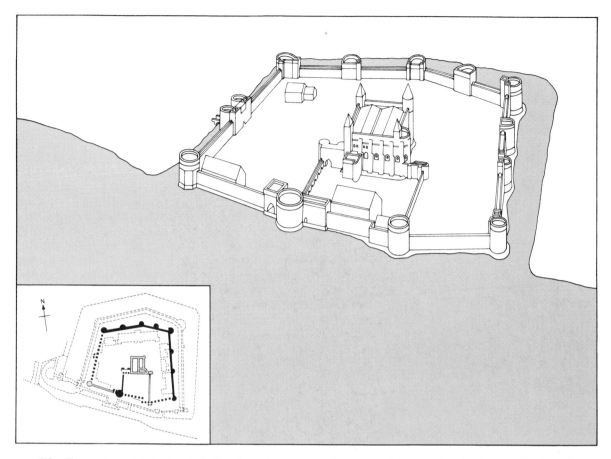

17 *The Tower in c.1270* (English Heritage).

forerunner of the Liberties, a strip of land to be kept free of buildings for the better defence of the Tower, was laid out. In 1261 Henry III wrote to his chief gardener commanding him to buy pear trees and plant them in this area 'which of late has been enclosed with a mud wall'.

Included in the area of the city taken in by the new circuit of walls was the parish church of St Peter ad Vincula, first mentioned in 1128–34, when it was already associated with the Tower. Henry considerably embellished the building, having large glazed windows inserted and stalls for himself and his queen placed in the nave with a great painted beam overhead bearing a Crucifix with John and Mary. All this appears to have been completed by December 1240 when, amongst other things, Henry ordered the two chancels to be wainscoted and a number of images of saints to be placed in the church.

The new defences, beginning at the Lanthorn Tower, extended east to the Salt Tower and so round the line of the inner wall to the Bell Tower. This effectively doubled the size of the castle and increased royal authority in the City at a time when the king's conflict with the barons was coming to a head. Most of this work, though much repaired and restored, still survives, with only two of the nine new towers (Brick and Flint) having been wholly rebuilt. All the towers are of cylindrical form with the largest and most impressive being located on the corners of the enclosure (Salt, Martin and Devereux towers). The height of these defences was seemingly increased during the subsequent works of Edward I, when the berm at the base of the walls was cut away and the foundations underpinned as part of the laying out of the Outer Ward. Nowhere is this better illustrated than on the south side of the Broad Arrow Tower, where an original postern in the curtain wall now lies some 2.8m (9 ft) above ground level (**18**).

18 *The small postern gate on the south side of the Broad Arrow Tower. Note the masonry underpinning below the gate, the top of which marks the line of the original ground level* (Historic Royal Palaces Agency).

Not long after this operation had begun a considerable setback occurred when, according to the contemporary chronicler, Matthew Paris, the 'stonework of a noble gate which the king had built at great expense' collapsed on the night of 23 April 1240 'as if struck by an earthquake'. Paris went on to state that in a second incident the new wall about the Tower also fell, exactly one year later at the same hour, an event which he fancifully attributed to the supernatural intervention of St Thomas Becket. The Elizabethan historian Stow (writing, of course, much later) identified the collapsed gate as being on the west side of the castle. The wall that suffered the same fate was probably a section of the adjacent curtain wall. There seems little doubt that the gate-tower stood on the site of the present Beauchamp Tower, and thus, as with earlier entrances, over the line of Great Tower Street, the western approach to the castle. It would also have stood close to the north-west angle of Longchamp's ditch and it is perhaps this, rather than divine retribution, which caused the gate-tower and wall to fall. It is perhaps relevant that examination of the footings of the late thirteenth-century curtain wall to the south of the Beauchamp Tower in 1958 (see **26**) found them to be of quite exceptional size and solidity – evidently Edward I's masons were determined to avoid the same fate that had overtaken Henry's gate-tower and wall.

The subsequent progress of Henry III's works is not easy to follow. Evidently the new defences were not complete by 1253 when the king ordered the constable to close a breach with timber palings. During the next few years, activity was considerably reduced owing to the adverse political and economic climate. But in 1261, after the king threw off the constraints of Simon de Montfort and the council of barons, work resumed in earnest. Again it is difficult to detail progress, but a reference to the building of a tower suggests that work on the outer wall was still in progress. During the civil war (1264–5) expenditure fell to almost nothing, but after 1267 work resumed and continued till the end of Henry's reign.

5

The apogee of the medieval castle under Edward I

Unlike his father, Edward I was a warrior king who had acquired his knowledge of the art of war campaigning on the continent of Europe and in the Holy Land. During his reign (1272–1307) the castle in England and Wales reached its apogee in architectural terms. The Tower of London, its defences already enlarged and modernized by Henry III, was further developed by Edward to become one of the greatest fortifications in the realm.

The majority of Edward's works were carried out between 1275 and 1285. The enormous scale of these operations is reflected in a recorded expenditure of some £21,000, more than twice that spent by Henry III on the castle during his entire reign. Doubtless Edward was involved in the outline planning, but the actual work was supervised by Master Robert of Beverley, who had directed operations at the Tower during the final years of the reign of Henry III, and a certain Brother John of the Order of St Thomas of Acre, significantly the only English military order in the Holy Land where castle design was more advanced than in Europe.

Edward's work involved the rebuilding of Henry III's western defences, the creation of a narrow outer ward and the construction of a complex western land entrance and great water-gate. The plan which resulted – a ring of defences within another – marked the ultimate expansion of the castle (19). Apart from a few subsequent additions and modifications, the plan of the defences in the late thirteenth century is essentially the plan that survives to this day.

The outer curtain wall and moat
The operation began with the excavation of the new moat. Between 1275 and 1281 no less than £4150 was spent on the wages of the diggers and hodmen alone (it has been calculated that the whole of a medium-sized castle at this time could have been constructed for about £1000!). In addition, tools had to be purchased, timber for shoring obtained and a Flemish engineer, a certain Master Walter, employed to ensure that, as with earlier works, the waters of the Thames were retained in the moat at low tide. Some of the clay from the excavations was used to infill that part of Henry III's ditch located behind the new wall. More was sold to the London tile-makers in an effort to offset some of the costs. When excavated, the moat was a more impressive feature than it now appears, since it was some 4.5m (15 ft) deeper in the centre, with the outer edge extending outwards to approximately the line of the present counterscarp wall (where the railings stand).

The accounts are surprisingly silent about the new curtain wall. It has long been supposed that as first planned the wall must have been comparatively low, not least because the formidable and contemporary firing gallery between the Bell and Devereux towers now looks out on to the back of the wall, rather than over it. A detailed inspection of the outer defences following recent cleaning, together with selective investigations, has enabled a phasing of the masonry to be attempted. The extent of the first phase is evidently represented by the top of the batter found just above the present level of the moat (20), which more or less equates with the late thirteenth-century ground surface within the Outer Ward. With some 2.6m (8 ft 6 ins) of masonry now buried, and allowing for a reasonable depth of parapet (presumably dismantled in advance of the heightening of the defences) a wall roughly 5m (17 ft) high can be postulated (21).

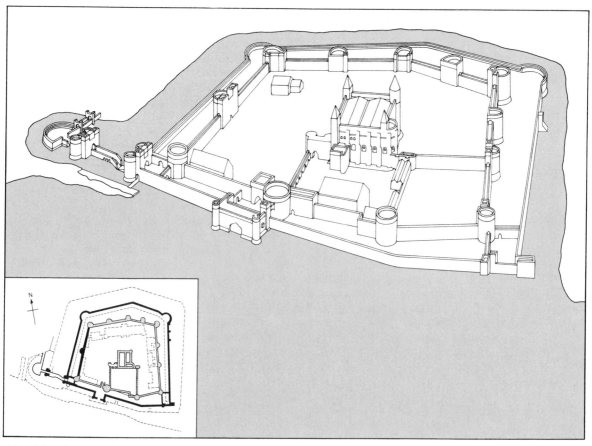

19 (*Above*) *The Tower in c.1300* (English Heritage).

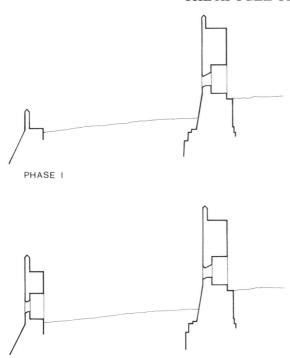

PHASE I

PHASE II

21 *Sketch sections through the western defences showing the suggested heightening of the outer curtain wall during the reign of Edward I* (English Heritage).

The main body of the wall is noticeably battered and must have served to retain the material used to infill Henry III's earlier ditch. Along the southern outer wall, within the Yeoman Warders' Club to the west of the Well Tower, there is evidence for a low arcaded wall above ground level carrying a wall-walk. This was incorporated into the broadening and heightening of the wall in 1326–9; the absence of similar evidence on the three landward sides might suggest that the arrangement along the riverside was more formidable, perhaps to compensate for the absence of a moat, which was not introduced here until the Wharf reached its full length late in the fourteenth century.

In short, therefore, Edward's Outer Ward formed a narrow corridor, which on the three

20 (*Left*) *The western defences showing the outer curtain wall and Legge's Mount with the Beauchamp Tower behind* (photo: Jeremy Hall, Royal Armouries).

landward sides was probably contained by a low revetment with the fire power of the castle concentrated along the walls and towers of the inner circuit. As such, this arrangement compares very closely with those found at two of Edward's great Welsh castles, Rhuddlan (begun 1277) and Harlech (begun 1283), and also the great castle of the Clares, the lords of Glamorgan, Caerphilly (begun 1271). There are other parallels drawn from Welsh castles to be found in the treatment of the north-east and north-west corners of the Outer Ward. These are covered by large bastions which have generally been described as late medieval or Tudor additions designed for artillery, though no documentary reference to support this has been found. Excavations in 1976 within Legge's Mount on the north-west corner (see **20**) indicated that it began life as an open-backed structure, its build apparently contemporary with that of the curtain wall. A subsequent excavation against the external junction with the curtain wall to the south confirmed that the two are indeed integral. In plan and dimensions Legge's Mount can be compared with the mounts on the corners of the outer wards at Caerphilly and Harlech. These are not towers as such, but roofless, semi-circular projections rising no higher than the adjoining walls.

The situation at the north-east corner of the Tower of London is more complex. Here building works in 1914 showed that the curtain wall originally formed an obtuse angle not covered by any structure. Immediately to the south, however, stood three small rectangular towers between 3m (10 ft) and 3.45m (11 ft 6 in) wide and set approximately 15m (50 ft) apart (**22**). Only the southernmost projection is now visible, the other two having been slighted after the moat was drained in 1843. When partly excavated in 1959–60 they were found to be of solid construction with impressive batters projecting and descending into the moat. Though not bonded into the wall, there is no reason to suppose that they are secondary, and it is perhaps significant that the Bembridge limestone (from the Isle of Wight) used to face the batters, is also employed consistently as quoins in the base of the curtain wall and Legge's Mount. As with Legge's Mount, it is probable that these projections rose no higher than the curtain wall. Their purpose is uncertain, but at this critical point it is possible that they were intended to accommodate stone-

22 *The most northerly of the three projections built against the eastern outer curtain wall during the reign of Edward I. Seen here from the battlements of the Brass Mount during excavations in 1981* (Author).

throwing devices – machines employed as much by defenders of castles as by their attackers.

St Thomas's Tower and the royal lodgings
To the south side of the Outer Ward was an area reclaimed from the river. The main water-gate of Henry III's time, the Bloody Tower, thus became an inner gate now approached by land. Consequently a new water entrance, St Thomas's Tower, was constructed immediately to the south, but on a far grander scale and incorporating splendid residential accommodation, evidently for the king himself, on the first floor (**23**). Built between 1275 and 1279, St Thomas's Tower has no architectural parallel in this country, but has been compared to the now vanished water-gate on the east front of

the Louvre in Paris (attributed to Philip Augustus, 1180–1223).

Below the great rear arch of St Thomas's Tower, notable for representing the largest single medieval span of its kind in the country, the water-filled basin originally extended to within some 3m (10 ft) of the Bloody Tower. This afforded spacious docking facilities behind the water entrance (Traitors' Gate) and needs to be compared with the restricted landward approach, with its narrow and awkward access to the Bloody Tower. Excavations in 1957 showed, however, that at some subsequent stage in the medieval period this constraint was alleviated by pushing the rear wall of the basin some 2m (6 ft) further to the south. The back of the basin was surrounded by a high wall pierced with arrow loops to cover the dock. The main gate in the wall, reached by a broad flight of steps, was located in front of the Bloody Tower (see **67**). Evidence suggests there was another, smaller gate in the north-east corner which probably provided direct access to the royal lodgings in St Thomas's Tower by means of a spiral staircase in the north-east tower. At

23 *Artist's impression of St Thomas's Tower and the water approach in the late Middle Ages* (Terry Ball).

ground-floor level the three walls of St Thomas's Tower contain mural passages that terminate either side of Traitors' Gate and provide access to small vaulted chambers in the south-east and south-west turrets. These passages are liberally pierced with arrow loops to cover the approach to the water entrance and the basin within.

When describing the lodgings on the first floor, the accounts refer to 'the great chamber towards the water of the Thames' and 'the hall with the chamber above the gate over the water of the Thames'. The palatial nature of the building is indicated by references to tiled floors, opening windows (a rare amenity at this date) containing coloured glass and painted statues set up on the riverside elevation. A

number of original features have been found during recent restoration work. These include the remains of two large fireplaces in the south wall (**24**) and a garderobe contrived in the west wall. The position of the latter can leave little doubt that the great chamber, the king's privy room, occupied the western half of the building, with the hall therefore to the east.

The mechanism to operate the great portcullis of the river entrance would not have been located on the first floor, but almost certainly on the roof. Of the two delightful small vaulted chambers in the corner turrets at first-floor level, that to the west, which during recent cleaning was found to have traces of yellow ochre on its ribs, perhaps functioned as a sort of strong-room off the great chamber. That to the east has traditionally been held to be a chapel because of the presence of two small basins cut into the window cills. However, such features abound in medieval buildings and more often

39

24 *Remains of the late thirteenth-century fireplace found in the eastern half of St Thomas's Tower* (photo: Garry Kennard, Royal Armouries).

than not are associated with ablutions, rather than prayer. Edward I, in his day one of the greatest rulers in Christendom and a man not known for doing things by half, might have regarded such a restricted space (in which an officiating priest could only just be accommodated) as not altogether adequate. Moreover, one might have expected a chapel to have been physically attached to the great chamber, in the same way that it was in Henry III's time in the Wakefield Tower. With these considerations in mind the precise function of the south-east chamber remains uncertain.

The suite in St Thomas's Tower was linked to the earlier royal lodgings by means of a bridge connecting the north-east turret with the upper chamber in the Wakefield Tower; the original disappeared during the eighteenth century, the present arrangement is a reconstruction of the 1860s (see **85**). It seems clear that the decision to establish the king's private apartments on the outer defences was motivated by geographic considerations within the enlarged fortress. The need to re-establish direct river access must have been a priority, though privacy and the unimpeded views that a location on the outer circuit offered were perhaps also important considerations.

Elsewhere along the new riverside curtain wall the forerunner of the Develin Tower was built on the eastern extremity and two small posterns formed. One stood immediately east of the Byward Tower, now rebuilt as the extant Byward Barbican. The other, to the east of St Thomas's Tower, probably on the site of the present Middle Drawbridge, was presumably intended to provide access to the heart of the palace complex. On either side of the fortress, where the ends of the moat entered the Thames, Edward had water-mills erected. Below that, towards the City there was also a stone wall 'to keep the water in the moat'. The origins of Tower Wharf also date from this time in the form of a comparatively short length of quay encased in timber extending from a point south-west of the Lion Tower to a point opposite the Byward Tower.

The western entrance
The new western entrance, complex and imposing, comprised an inner and outer gatehouse, with a massive barbican beyond, all linked by stone causeways incorporating drawbridge pits (**colour plate 3**). The barbican, which has a marked similarity to the contemporary entrance of Goodrich Castle, was known as the Lion Tower because of its long association with the king's beasts. This great half-moon-shaped firing platform was surrounded by a stone-lined moat and approached via a causeway to the north. This was rediscovered and excavated in 1936 and together with its drawbridge pit and recesses for counter-balance weights is now on display. Access on to the causeway was formerly controlled by a small spur-gate which

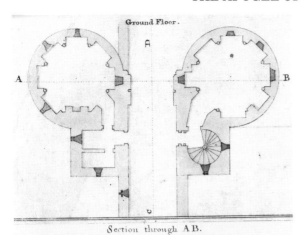

Ground Floor.

Section through A B.

Section through C D.

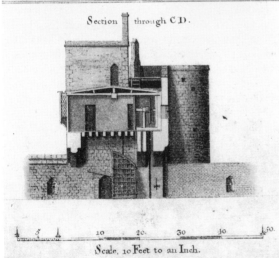

Scale, 10 Feet to an Inch.

25 *Plan and sections of the Middle Tower in advance of the restorations of 1717–19. Drawn by Clement Lemprière, 1717* (Public Record Office).

can be seen on the 1597 survey labelled 'The Lyons Gate' (see **36**). As for the Lion Tower itself, the lower half now lies buried beneath the present roadway and the utilitarian Victorian building that houses the Tower shop.

Beyond stands the Middle Tower, the outer twin-towered gatehouse. The exterior was partly resurfaced in Portland stone during the early eighteenth century, but within it much medieval fabric remains, including fine stone vaults to the ground-floor rooms (**25**). The interior walls are lined with brick, part of the remarkable early use of this material by Edward I at the Tower. The long causeway linking the Middle Tower with the Byward Tower has a noticeable kink in its plan, presumably intended to hinder any attack along its course. The causeway originally carried high parapet walls pierced with arrow loops to cover the water to the north and south, but only the lower half of the south wall now survives, having been cut down early in the nineteenth century.

So to the Byward Tower – the inner gatehouse. Larger and loftier than the otherwise similarly designed Middle Tower, this now carries an additional second floor of late medieval or Tudor date. Between the turrets to the rear, the tops of which again display the early use of brick, the back of the tower is, and always was, timber framed. Standing within the gatepassage the visitor can easily appreciate the strength of a fully developed Edwardian gatehouse, with rebates for a portcullis both front and rear of the great gates and arrow loops covering the foreground from the towers either side. Despite their name, the murder holes in the arch above were probably intended to douse fires against the gates, rather than channel boiling oil on the heads of attackers as is popularly believed. In addition to retaining its forward portcullis the Byward Tower also still possesses the machinery to lift it (**26**). Though not original, the carpentry appears to date from the later Middle Ages, and as such represents a very rare device. The first floor of the tower also retains the most important medieval decorative interiors in the castle. Much dates from the late fourteenth century (see below), but the walls in the north tower show traces of an earlier false ashlar scheme painted red on a white background, while the chamber over the gate passage retains vestiges of an original late thirteenth-century patterned tile pavement.

In 1281 the accounts specifically refer to the completion of the wall between the Bell and Devereux towers and the building of the Beauchamp Tower mid-way along its length. The Beauchamp Tower occupies the site of Henry

26 *The Byward Tower windlass and portcullis* (Historic Royal Palaces Agency).

III's western entrance and it is significant that in plan the walls either side do not form a straight line (**27** and **colour plate 4**). This suggests that Henry's gate was still in use until the new entrance was ready (in the summer of 1281) and that its presence visually barred the laying out of the inner western curtain on a single line. The cleaning of the interior of the Beauchamp Tower revealed that the brick facing, previously thought to be a post-medieval resurfacing, is in fact original. A close examination of the adjoining walls, including the formidable row of embrasures and loops which survive in the basements and cellars of the abutting sixteenth- and seventeenth-century buildings, revealed them to be of identical construction. The bricks can be identified in the building accounts for 1276–8, as 228,300 'quarell de Flandr' purchased from one John Bardown of Ypres in modern Belgium. They were bought by the long hundred (six score = 120) so that the actual figure can be increased to 243,000. The use of nearly a quarter of a million bricks at this time is without precedent and represents the first major use of this material in England since the demise of the

Roman Empire. The figure becomes even more impressive when, as seems certain, another 120,000 bricks were purchased in 1283 for the wall between the Tower and the City.

The Postern Gate
Another building where the early use of brick has been observed is the Postern Gate at the southern end of the City defences overlooking the Tower moat. The gate, as its name indicates, was a subsidiary entrance into London for pedestrian traffic. The earliest surviving reference to the building dates from 1308. Though the City was responsible for manning and maintaining the building throughout its history, the Crown was almost certainly responsible for its construction, not least because the excavation of Edward I's moat would have left the end of the City wall broken and undefended. According to the Chronicle of William Gregory disaster struck the postern in 1431, when on 17 July it 'sanke downe into the erthe vii fote and more'. Stow adds that it was never properly rebuilt, but that a wooden structure was raised on the ruins which was 'inhabited by persons of lewd life'. The unexpected discovery of the remains of the postern, during the excavation of a subway into the moat gardens in 1978, provided confirmation of the historical accounts (**28**). The excavated structure was clearly displaced and occupied an uncomfortable angle. Originally comprising three floors, the basement and the lower parts of the ground floor and the gate-passage to the north survived and are now on display.

Entry into the gate-passage was controlled by a portcullis and gate. Within the passage is a short wall attached to the tower containing an arrow loop (**29**). This highly unusual feature was intended to cover the entrance and restrict movement in the narrow passage. The basement had been infilled during the sixteenth century when a series of mean brick walls was erected on the site. Parts of a fine vault were recovered from the infilling which probably came from the first-floor chamber. The finds included a hollowed-out roof boss which appeared to be strikingly similar to a well-dated mid-fourteenth-century group from within the Tower and Windsor Castle. If the attribution is correct then it might be that the gatehouse was refurbished at an early date, perhaps due to the subsidence that ultimately brought about the building's downfall.

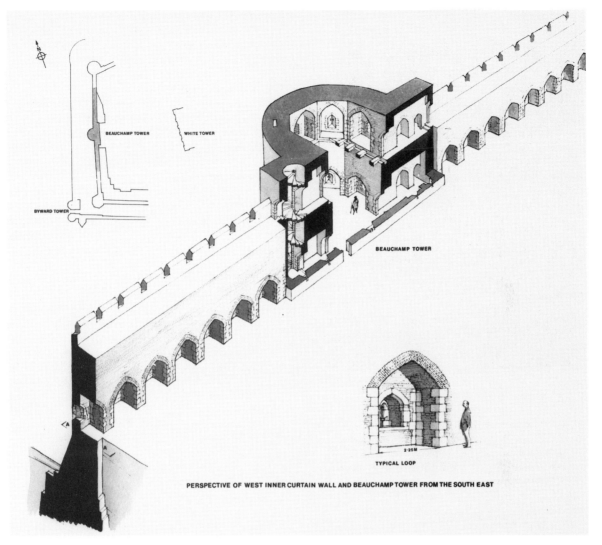

BEAUCHAMP TOWER

WHITE TOWER

BYWARD TOWER

BEAUCHAMP TOWER

TYPICAL LOOP

2·25M

PERSPECTIVE OF WEST INNER CURTAIN WALL AND BEAUCHAMP TOWER FROM THE SOUTH EAST

27 *Cut-away perspective of western inner curtain wall and Beauchamp Tower* (Terry Ball).

The outer defences strengthened

There remains one major addition to the defences of the Tower which, though seemingly undocumented, must belong to the reign of Edward I, that is the heightening of the outer landward defences (see **21**). The work was probably associated with the decision to relocate the Mint within the walls of the Tower. The circumstances under which this occurred are not known, but in the Pipe Roll for 1279–81 an expenditure of £79 17s 8½d is recorded on buildings and equipment at the Tower. There are references to 'the little tower where the treasure of the mint is kept' and to timber

bought 'for the workshops in the barbecan'. There is no evidence for exact locations, but the reference to the barbican might equate more readily with the Lion Tower at the western entrance, rather than a site in the Outer Ward.

In March 1300, the number of furnaces at the Tower was increased to 30, for which the Mint Warden, John Dandale, was ordered to erect a building 400 ft long. There can be little doubt that the building was erected in the Outer Ward, and that by this date the walls had been heightened to afford protection. In fact the walls were carried up to more or less their present height, as evidenced by the recent discovery of a series of blocked crenellations on the south side of Legge's Mount. It is worth noting that these features represent the only

28 *The remains of the Postern Gate looking south-east during excavation in 1979* (Historic Royal Palaces Agency).

known medieval battlements to survive at the Tower, for all the rest are nineteenth-century reconstructions. Early nineteenth-century views of the Tower show a continuous moulding around the edges of these crenellations (**colour plate 4**). These may have been similar to the cope mouldings found on the battlements of the Eagle Tower at Caernarvon Castle, built in 1285–91.

Legge's Mount appears to have been raised to a level slightly above the adjoining walls, but otherwise remained an open-backed feature.

On the north-east corner the heightening was accompanied by the addition of Brass Mount, whose structure partly displaced the most northern of the three small towers built against the wall during the first phase of Edward I's work. Projecting somewhat more boldly into the moat than Legge's Mount, Brass Mount appears also to have been unenclosed to begin with, but contains a formidable firing gallery in the thickness of the masonry (**30**) reminiscent of that found in the inner west curtain wall. Furthermore, the passage, together with its associated garderobes, is lined with original brick. It is tempting to equate the use of this material with 120,000 bricks ordered for the outer curtain wall in 1283. If the association is

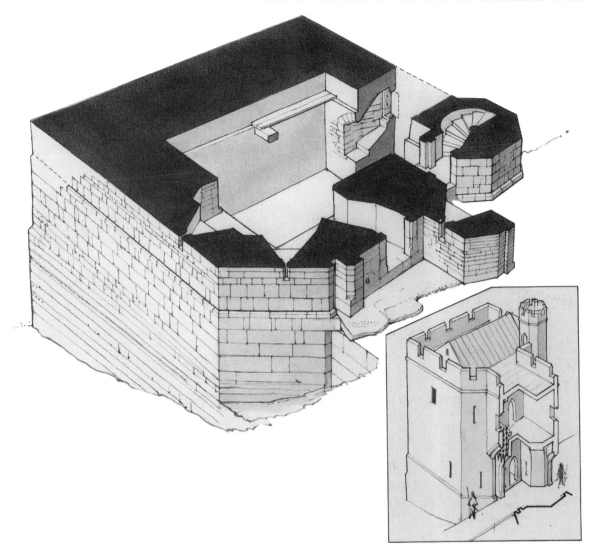

29 *Cut-away illustration of the remains of the Postern Gate and* (insert) *a suggested reconstruction* (Terry Ball).

correct, there can have been no appreciable interval between the initial construction of the outer defences and the decision to heighten the walls and remodel the north-east corner. The likelihood of this is perhaps further supported by the nature of the masonry which, with the exception of the two different types of stone used to form the quoins in the upper and lower parts of the wall, is indistinguishable. Finally, it is worth noting that the quoins show ample evidence for a false ashlar design chiselled on their faces (**31**). This indicates that the walls

were intended to be whitewashed, for if so treated the large stone blocks would visually merge with the coursed rubble.

There were other, subsidiary, defences provided by Edward I in the Outer Ward to give added protection to entry points into the castle. These can still be identified on the 1597 survey in the form of cross walls and gates – two located to the south and west of the Bell Tower, a pair either side of St Thomas's Tower and another two attached to the south and east sides of the Salt Tower (see **36**). One of the few remaining sections of these walls is to be found on the south side of the Salt Tower, where it connects with the Well Tower. Though not identifiable in the accounts, the Well Tower is

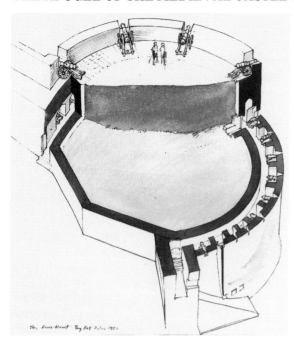

30 *Cut-away illustration of the Brass Mount as it might have appeared in 1683 after the introduction of guns into the mural passage* (Terry Ball).

also probably the work of Edward I and the ground floor contains an original stone vault of thirteenth-century form. It is interesting to note the discovery in this chamber in 1974 of two stone-lined chutes in the south wall; evidently intended for drawing water from the river, their presence would seem to indicate the origins of the building's name.

Lastly, the non-military and more domestic aspects of the castle were not neglected under Edward I. The Chapel of St Peter ad Vincula, repaired by Henry III, was rebuilt by Edward I at a cost of £317 8s 3d between 17 June 1286

31 *Detail of false ashlar cut into the quoins of Legge's Mount* (Author).

and 6 April 1287. Various improvements were carried out in the palace and the king's gardens were planted with, amongst other things, five hundred willows and one hundred cherry trees while the slopes of Tower Hill were terraced with vines and fruit trees.

6

The later medieval period

Whereas several writers have asserted that the works undertaken by Edward I represent the last additions of any importance to the medieval castle, it would be absurd to suggest that its architectural development had ended. Succeeding fourteenth- and fifteenth-century monarchs repaired and improved the lines of defences and sought to modernize the domestic accommodation within.

The only important contribution by Edward II (1307–27) was the rebuilding 'broader and higher' of the southern outer curtain wall from St Thomas's Tower eastwards towards St Katherine's in 1324–5. Otherwise it would appear that Edward II neglected the Tower, as a list of dilapidations drawn up in 1335, and the very extensive reparations that followed it, indicate.

The works of Edward III
Edward III (1327–77) was a great builder and not the sort of monarch who would allow one of his principal fortresses to fall into disrepair. Most of his building operations were associated with further improvements to the river front, beginning in 1336 with a resumption of work on the southern outer curtain wall – perhaps made all the more important by the outbreak of the Hundred Years' War and the threat posed by French water-borne incursions. This work involved the heightening and widening of the wall from St Thomas's Tower to the Byward Tower. Edward I's postern adjacent to the Byward Tower was refashioned, but subsequently demolished in 1342 and rebuilt as a tower in 1350. This still stands, together with a small porter's lodge to the west, as part of the extant Byward Barbican remodelled by Henry VIII.

The entire length of the southern inner curtain wall between the Bell and Salt Towers was heightened and crenellated in 1339, while a stout gatehouse was constructed in the wall midway between the Lanthorn and Salt towers in 1339–41 (**colour plate 5**). Between 1348 and 1355 a new privy water-gate for the king, the present Cradle Tower, was built on the river curtain immediately to the south-west – the Black Death evidently delaying its completion. This now stands as the principal surviving building of Edward III's time at the Tower, though the top floor dates from the 1870s, the original having been removed in 1776. A handsome building, the ground floor comprises a central gate passage with a small chamber on either side (**32**). That to the east, heated by a small fireplace, must have acted as the porter's lodge, the other formed a vestibule to the royal apartments reached from here by the spiral staircase in the south-west corner and by means of a bridge spanning the Outer Ward to the Lanthorn Tower (compare with St Thomas's Tower). All three rooms are vaulted, with the ribs springing from an interesting group of corbels featuring animal grotesques. The cleaning of these vaults in 1990 revealed traces of red ochre on the ribs, a reminder of the ubiquitous use of colour in medieval buildings.

It has been suggested that the Cradle Tower and the gatehouse to the north formed part of a new access to the palace that was rendered desirable by the king's decision to transfer his private apartment to chambers in and around the Lanthorn Tower. Whereas the Cradle Tower undoubtedly was associated with this development, the impetus for the gate-tower may have been linked to the construction of a major stone building against the east side of the

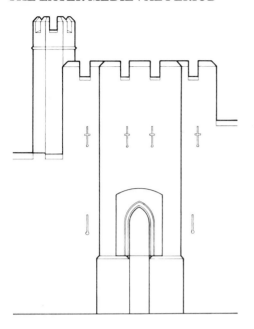

SOUTH ELEVATION

NORTH ELAVATION

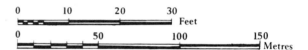

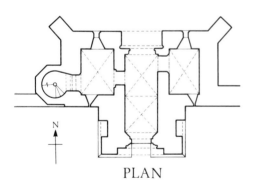

PLAN

32 *Ground plan and elevations of the Cradle Tower* (English Heritage).

White Tower, possibly to accommodate the royal wardrobe. This building can be identified on the 1597 survey as a long rectangular structure with an internal courtyard – a form it substantially retained until its eventual demolition in 1879 (see **83**). In 1821 the historian John Bayley attributed the building to Edward III, through no documentary reference to it can now be found. There can be little doubt that its origins were medieval and that it was erected after the limits of the castle had been pushed eastwards during the reign of Henry III, not

least because the east face of the building lay beyond the line of the Roman city wall. Information obtained from an excavation in 1954, together with observations made during works in 1974, suggest that the robbing of the Roman city wall at this point was carried out during the construction of the building and pottery evidence indicates that this occurred no earlier than the fourteenth century.

Other works to the southern defences carried out during the reign of Edward III may include the building of a new postern entrance over the south-east corner of the moat to replace the forerunner of the Develin Tower and mill (or mills) erected there by Edward I (**colour plate 5**). The new arrangement evidently comprised a walled causeway commanded outwardly by a simple gate-tower, known as the Iron Gate, and inwardly by the Develin Tower. The Iron Gate

33 *The Develin Tower on the south-east corner of the outer defences. A former entrance into the castle for pedestrian and pack-horse traffic* (photo: Jeremy Hall, Royal Armouries).

and causeway were demolished in 1680. The Develin Tower still stands and though much altered the north face of the building exhibits a good deal of original medieval masonry which, comprised of small, squared, rubble is characteristically fourteenth century in nature (**33**). Similar masonry can be identified in the upper part of the south curtain wall between the Develin Tower and Well Tower, suggesting that this area of masonry was refashioned at the same time.

A further small but interesting exercise undertaken in Edward III's time is the vault of the gateway through the Bloody Tower which is still extant. Carried out under contract by Robert (brother of the more famous Henry) Yevele between 1360 and 1362, it comprises an unusual set of lions' masks within bosses. A recently discovered fourteenth-century tiled

pavement in the chamber above possibly dates from the same refurbishment and indicates a residential use of some grandeur.

The Tower Wharf was another feature that received considerable attention during Edward III's reign. The comparatively short quay created by Edward I between Petty Wales and the Byward Tower was extended in c.1338–9, again in timber and earth, as far as St Thomas's Tower. Between 1365 and 1370 the builders returned to encase the whole in stone.

Finally, Edward's reign witnessed certain repairs and amendments to residential buildings within the Tower. These included in 1336 the heightening and re-roofing of the great hall, together with the renewal of the windows in the north wall. Between 1354 and 1356 a new house for the king's chaplain was built and between 1361 and 1366 another for the constable at considerable expense. The house probably replaced the constable's earlier lodgings and occupied the site of the present Queen's House where much medieval masonry is to be found embedded in the sixteenth-century structure (**34 and 35**). Indeed, the medieval remains partly determine the plan of the southern range; the eastern gable wall, for example, appears to be medieval as far up as the roof.

The concluding works of the Middle Ages
During Richard II's reign (1377–99) the major work undertaken at the Tower involved a further extension of Tower Wharf. Carried out during the last decade of the fourteenth century, while Geoffrey Chaucer was Clerk of the Works, this saw the quay extended the full length of the riverside to assume the form it retains to this day. The completed embankment, which incorporated a tunnel or bridge in front of the river entrance to St Thomas's Tower, which became known as Traitors' Bridge, is depicted for the first time in a fifteenth-century painting at the British Museum (**colour plate 1**).

The only other notable piece of building work carried out in Richard II's time was the construction of a house for John Ludewyk, Keeper of the Privy Wardrobe from 1396 to 1399. It is tempting to see this building as the later Jewel House, shown against the south face of the White Tower in the 1597 survey – not least because the slender tower at the west end might have been the 'Ludwyktoure' referred to

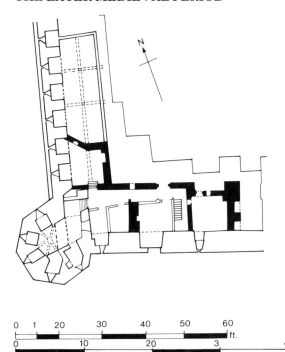

34 *(Above) Ground plan of the Queen's House showing (in solid form) the remains of the medieval constable's lodgings* (English Heritage).

in a document of 1399. It has been suggested that the need for a new Jewel House may have been brought about during the Peasant's Revolt when a crowd somehow entered the Tower unopposed and looted Richard II's wardrobe.

To the end of the fourteenth century can be attributed the remarkable painting of the Crucifixion discovered in 1953 on the south wall of the chamber over the Byward Tower gate passage. Sadly mutilated by the insertion of a fireplace in the sixteenth century, the mural is now missing the central depiction of Christ, but images of the Virgin and the Saints either side attest to the fine quality of the work (**colour plate 6**). The main ceiling beam overhead is richly decorated with gold fleurs-de-lis, leopards and heraldic birds on a green background. This pattern almost certainly extended over the whole of the ceiling and can also be found in the background of the wall painting,

35 *(Below) Part of the remains of the medieval constable's lodgings still to be found in the Queen's House* (Historic Royal Palaces Agency).

thus indicating that the two are contemporary.

During the reign of Edward IV (1461–83) a notable, but seemingly ill-documented piece of work was the construction of the Bulwark on Tower Hill at the western entrance (**colour plate 7**). Evidently designed for artillery, it might be supposed that guns were mounted on two cylindrical bastions located at the head of the enclosure – one covering Great Tower Street, the other the approach down the hill and the main entrance into the enclosure. Rescue excavations on Tower Hill in advance of drainage works in 1985, revealed evidence for the plan of the enclosure which, hitherto, was known only from picturesque sixteenth- and seventeenth-century bird's-eye surveys. The masonry was of brick construction throughout, including numerous contemporary, or near contemporary, buildings that crowded against the inner face of the defences. The function of all these structures is not clear, though it is worth noting that a certain Thomas Redhede, appointed to the office of Porter of the Tower of London and Keeper of 'le bulwark' in March 1484, was provided with a mansion within the said enclosure.

7

Functions of the medieval castle

Like any castle the Tower of London was the fortified residence of its lord. That the lord was the king of England and the fortress located within the capital of the realm elevated its importance above most. It was, in effect, the principal castle of medieval England and as the peripatetic nature of royal government changed, the Tower became home to various institutions which have evolved down to the present day.

The castle as a royal stronghold
The maintenance of the Tower's fortifications was a primary concern of royal government, not only for defensive reasons, but for offensive ones as well. Numerous surviving medieval accounts of heroic sieges tend to make the defensive role of the castle the primary one, but castles performed the arguably more important role of providing secure bases from which campaigns could be mounted and surrounding districts subjugated. The statement by Stow in 1598 that 'This tower is a Citadell, to defend or commaund the Citie' illustrates that as far as the Tower of London was concerned the military duality persisted long after the close of the era known as the Middle Ages. The need for the Crown to control London, which during the medieval period was governed by a small, elite merchant oligarchy, was paramount from the time of the Norman invasion. Tension was never far away and the City often led the way in challenging royal authority, as happened during the reign of Henry III when it provided the power base for Simon de Montfort.

From its foundation, the residential aspects of the Tower were of great importance, and the Conqueror's White Tower represented a fortified palatial stone donjon that was to influence the design of keeps elsewhere in England for over one hundred years. There is little evidence for the following development of the royal lodgings until the works of Henry III, during whose reign the principal palace facilities were firmly established within the bailey south of the White Tower. Apart from some additions and modifications the complex established at this time was to endure until the start of the sixteenth century and the improvements of Henry VII which belong to another age.

It is perhaps ironic that three of the monarchs most associated with the development of the Tower, William I, Henry III and Edward I, should have spent so little time there. In the case of the Conqueror there is no evidence that he ever saw his great White Tower, let alone stayed in it. As for Henry III, in the 45 years between 1227 (the end of his minority) and 1272 (his death) there are only eleven recorded cases of the king going to the Tower. Collectively these account for 32 weeks, but most were taken up in lengthy stays in 1261, 1263 and 1272. Excluding these years, the king visited the Tower only twice in 42 years, and then only for a total of about seven days. Records show that Henry preferred to stay at Westminster and visits to the Tower were confined to periods of political crisis. Edward I came even less. He also preferred the more open surroundings of Westminster, though he also spent time at York House, the residence of the Archbishop of York in the City.

By comparison, King John, who appears to have had little to do with the physical evolution of the Tower, made about 22 visits between 1204 and 1216. What these examples show is that royal occupation was irregular and patchy and that generally speaking the Tower was a place where monarchs tended to go when they wanted to project themselves in a forceful manner.

During the later medieval period the Tower singularly failed to protect some of its royal owners. In 1381 Richard II was besieged in the castle by the peasants who had marched on London from Essex and Kent. While the young king rode to Mile End to meet Wat Tyler some of the rebels managed to enter the fortress unopposed. The Archbishop of Canterbury, Simon of Sudbury, and others, sought sanctuary in the Chapel of St John in the White Tower, but were dragged away and beheaded on Tower Hill. The rebels also looted the armoury and Jewel House and broke into the royal apartments where one chronicler claimed some 'arrogantly lay and sat on the king's bed while joking; and several asked the king's mother to kiss them'. In 1399, after Henry Bolingbroke returned from exile, Richard was taken prisoner to the Tower and it was in the White Tower that he declared his abdication.

In 1460 the Tower held out against a Yorkist siege, during which its walls were damaged by artillery, but was forced to surrender after the Lancastrian Henry VI was captured at Northampton. The deposed Henry briefly recovered his throne in 1470 with the aid of the Earl of Warwick. Edward IV quickly regained the upper hand, however, and returned Henry to the Tower where he was probably murdered.

The development of the Wardrobe and other institutions

Like other European rulers, Norman monarchs moved ceaselessly about the realm on business, with a small army of officials, servants, armed retainers and all their possessions, rarely staying more than a few nights in any one location. Strong-rooms were established in the various royal castles and manors where the king's robes, jewels, ornaments, coined money, books, accounts, arms and armour, and even items of furniture could be stored with safety. The movement of all this luggage, known as the wardrobe, was not surprisingly a matter of great concern to the king, and the staff assigned to administer it steadily increased as time went by. In due course the transportation of the itinerant wardrobe was found to be very inconvenient, and as a consequence the practice of storing it in special buildings came about.

The stationary part of the wardrobe department, which spent its energies in acquiring and holding stock, became known as the great wardrobe and attained independence from its parent organization in 1253, under Roger de Ros the king's tailor. Subsequently this body fragmented, with one portion concentrating on raw materials, cloth and the business of tailoring, while the other concerned itself with the king's personal property, including arms. The latter, the privy wardrobe, itself became more specialized and eventually yet another division occurred when the arsenal branch became the privy wardrobe at the Tower in July 1323 – not least because by then the great wardrobe munitions section was located in the Tower. It was not until 1360 that the Tower establishment severed all its ties, both financially and administratively, from the privy wardrobe, but even before then it was effectively responsible for the purchase, storage and maintenance of all manner of stores of war, including guns and ammunition.

In 1414 a new chapter was opened in the Patent Rolls with the appointment of Nicholas Merbury as 'Master of the works of the King's engines and of the ordnance'. This marks the birth of the Office of Ordnance, an organization that was to become a major department of state during the sixteenth century and which was to initiate a system of armament administration which has persisted down to the present day. The position the Office came to occupy in administering large areas of the Tower can be traced back to the middle of the fifteenth century when, in 1452, the Master of the Ordnance, Thomas Vaughan, successfully petitioned the king for use of all that part of the Wharf between Traitors' Bridge and St Katherine's to the east.

The Office of Ordnance was not the only settled institution to emerge from within the walls of the medieval Tower. The establishment of the Mint in the Outer Ward during the reign of Edward I saw the start of over five hundred years of coin production at the Tower, though, with the exception of some fragments of late medieval vessels carrying traces of gold and silver which were found in Legge's Mount in 1976, physical evidence for the medieval operations remains elusive. By the time of Edward I important records of state were also being held in the castle and in 1312 racks were purchased to store the documents on. During the following reign of Edward II instructions were given as to how the record rolls should be sorted and arranged. Where these documents, which by then are known to have been kept in chests, were held is not known, but in 1360 the Chancery records were evidently transferred from the White Tower to a building elsewhere within the walls to make way for King John of France and other distinguished prisoners.

Perhaps one of the most unlikely institutions to be established within the medieval Tower was the Royal Menagerie. The earliest record of exotic animals being kept there dates from 1235, when Henry III was presented with three leopards by his brother-in-law, the Emperor Frederick II. Seventeen years later a white polar bear arrived from Norway and the sheriffs of London were ordered to pay 4d a day for the maintenance of the animal (and its keeper) and to provide a chain and a long stout cord to hold it while it was fishing in the Thames.

In 1255 Henry III was to receive his most exotic beast – an elephant presented by Louis IX of France. Again the sheriffs of London were called upon – this time to pay for the construction of an elephant house 40 ft long and 20 ft wide. The warrant added that they were to build the house in such a way that it could be used for something else, thus after the animal died in 1257 a reference to a Jewess 'in the Elephant House' indicates that it had been utilized as a prison.

It was, however, the lions that were to capture the public imagination and references to them at the Tower in the fourteenth and fifteenth centuries are relatively frequent. Under Edward II it was laid down that each lion should receive a quarter of mutton a day and his keeper 3½d. By the reign of Edward III the keeper's wage had risen to 12d a day, while 12d a day was allowed for the animal's food. The exact site of the menagerie throughout the medieval period is not known.

Early prisoners

The function which, above all others, has captured the public's imagination is the Tower as a state prison. As centres of local government, there can scarcely be a castle in England which has not been used as a prison at one time or another, though few performed the role on anything like a regular basis. The Tower, however, the strongest fortress in London, was from the earliest period seen as a secure and convenient place to hold state prisoners. Ranulf

Flambard, Bishop of Durham, is the earliest recorded prisoner, having been sent there on the orders of Henry I in 1100.

No part of the Tower was specifically built as a prison and no part was ever consistently used in this way. Most buildings probably served as a prison lodging at some time or other. Where a person was kept depended on his rank. Thus the White Tower, beginning with Flambard, occasionally held some of the most famous, including the Welsh prince Gruffyd, who fell to his death while trying to escape from there in 1244. King John of France was lodged there in 1359 and Charles, Duke of Orleans, who was held in various English castles between 1415 and 1440, had his stay in the White Tower depicted in a miniature illustration of the late fifteenth century (**colour plate 1**). Most prisoners, however, were probably held in the wall towers which offered spacious and secure accommodation where noble and other persons of rank could reside with their servants. For the medieval period there is no evidence for the habit of sixteenth- and seventeenth-century prisoners of carving graffiti on the walls.

Perhaps the largest group of prisoners held within the medieval Tower were the Jews. During the reigns of Henry III and Edward I large numbers were incarcerated from all over the country after failing to pay special taxes levied on them. During the early reign of Edward I it is said that 600 Jews were crowded together in the sub-crypt of the White Tower. At times, however, the Jews of London were brought to the Tower for their own protection, such as on the occasion of Henry III's re-coronation at Westminster in 1220, when the king's ministers recalling the anti-Jewish riots that erupted at Richard I's coronation, had the entire community locked up within the walls. It was, in fact, the constable of the Tower who exercised both civil and criminal jurisdiction over the Jews of London, and the quarter of the City in which they lived, the Jewry, was in effect a liberty of the Tower. The reason for this can be found in the nature of the medieval Jewish community in England. It was the early Norman kings who, for financial reasons, introduced the Jews into England from Normandy. Because of the king's interest they were treated as dependants of the Crown and protected by the Crown's officers who regulated and supervised their business transactions up until the time of their expulsion in 1290.

8

The early Tudors

The only significant works undertaken during the reign of Henry VII were by way of improvements to the ageing royal palace. The three major items revealed in the chamber accounts are the construction of a new gallery and tower and the laying out of a garden. Work on the new tower, which housed the king's library, began in 1502. It appears to have stood in the region of the Lanthorn Tower and may have been the slender tower which can be seen on the outer wall to the west of the Cradle Tower on the 1597 survey (referred to as Queen Elizabeth's Tower or the Brick Tower in later accounts). Alternatively it may have been the gatehouse spanning the Outer Ward between the slender tower and the Lanthorn Tower, thus representing a replacement of the earlier arrangement of Edward III (**36**). The gallery, a timber-framed structure with plastered exterior, was constructed along the top of the curtain wall between the Lanthorn Tower and Salt Tower. The garden was probably the Privy Garden lying to the south of the gallery or the larger Wardrobe Garden to the north.

The reign of Henry VIII
Evidently during the reign of Henry VIII the barbican immediately east of the Byward Tower was remodelled by adding the wedge-shaped projection towards the Wharf. This is pierced at ground-floor level by two small gun ports (one in the east flank the other in the salient). These are the earliest known features of their kind at the Tower and were designed to accommodate small pieces of ordnance mounted on stocks (hollowed-out pieces of wood) rather than wheeled carriages. Of further interest is the form of a loop with double key-holes for hand guns at a higher level in the

east face. It was Henry VIII who in 1519–20 had the Chapel of St Peter ad Vincula rebuilt, following a fire in 1512. The existing building, albeit extensively refurbished in the nineteenth century, dates from this time. Also dating from c.1510–20 was the remodelling and enlarging, in brick, hence its name, of the thirteenth-century Brick Tower along the northern inner curtain wall, as a residence for the Master of the Ordnance.

In 1532 a general repair of the Tower's defences was set in motion by Thomas Cromwell. This was preceded by a detailed survey which indicates that virtually every tower and every intervening stretch of wall was in need of some attention. It was estimated that 2937 tons of Caen stone would be needed and that the total cost of the works would be £3593 4s 1d. A good deal of work was done to the White Tower, including the installation of new lead-covered cupolas on the four turrets to replace earlier, conical shaped devices which can be seen on a late fifteenth-century miniature. The Tudor cupolas still exist, though the great weather vanes that surmounted them, which were decorated by the Italian painter Ellys Carmyan, were replaced in 1668 (see below, p. 69).

At St Thomas's Tower the timber framing was taken down and rebuilt according to a contract with the master carpenter, Thomas Nedeham, for £120. The existing timberwork, though repaired, and with the three great oriel windows in the north front now replaced by nineteenth-century reconstructions, dates from this period. The roof is very heavily framed and there can be little doubt that it was designed to withstand the weight of guns. At the time of the Wyatt rebellion in 1554 there is mention of three guns being mounted 'on the Watergate'

55

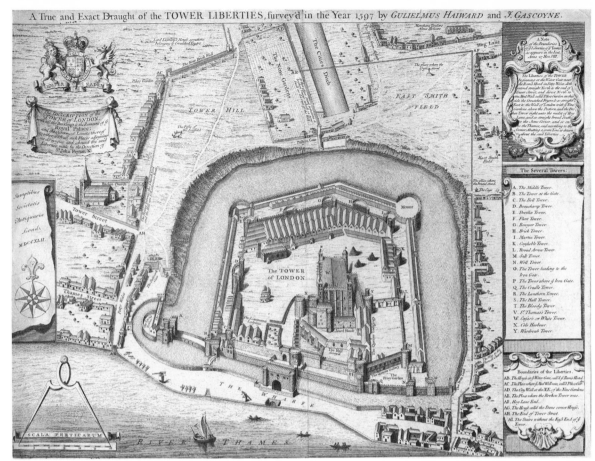

36 *Survey of the Tower and its Liberties by Haiward and Gascoyne, 1597* (English Heritage).

and ten years later there is a reference to replacing a gun platform on the roof of the building. Nedeham's work at St Thomas's also included building a small house 6 by 5m (20 by 17 ft), of unknown function, against the north-west corner. The house can be identified on the 1735 survey resting on piers rising from within the water-filled basin (see **67**). These piers still survive below the present level of Water Lane, where they are incorporated into some sort of nineteenth-century drainage chamber. The masonry is apparently late medieval in date and presumably supported a forerunner of Nedeham's building.

It was, however, in the royal lodgings that the most important works were undertaken, all of which were completed in time for Henry VIII and Ann Boleyn to lodge there the night before her coronation in May 1533. The King's Gallery, erected by Henry VII between the Salt Tower and Lanthorn Tower, was repaired, together with the Council Chamber over Edward III's gatehouse half way along its length. Elsewhere in the king's lodgings works were carried out in the Great Watching Chamber, Great Chamber, Dining (i.e. Presence) Chamber, Closet and Privy Chamber, all of which were concentrated in and about the Lanthorn Tower. Within the queen's side to the north the principal works were to the great chamber, which was given a new roof and floor, and the Dining Chamber, which was entirely rebuilt. It is worth mentioning that work on the private apartments saw the introduction, albeit in a limited form, of classical decoration in the castle. Elsewhere a new garden was laid out for the queen on the south side of the King's Gallery, and another for the king to the north. A new timber-framed wardrobe measuring 31 by 7m (101 by 24 ft) was built as a range between the Wardrobe Tower and Broad Arrow

Old Houses, adjoining the Bloody Tower Tower of London now pulled down for the improvements Sep. 1846

37 *Row of seven timber-framed buildings erected against the curtain wall north of the Wakefield Tower in 1533. A drawing by T. H. Shepherd made shortly before the buildings were taken down in September 1846 (Guildhall Library).*

Tower (see **36**), while a row of seven 'houses of offices' was constructed against the west face of the curtain wall running south from Coldharbour Gate (**37**).

The celebrations connected with Anne's coronation were accompanied by the creation of no less than sixty Knights of the Bath. This entailed further works, including the repair and redecoration of Henry III's great hall, the overhaul of the kitchens and the partitioning of the new accommodation in St Thomas's Tower to provide lodgings for the Lord Great Chamberlain and the Lord Chamberlain.

In the wake of Anne's coronation, James Nedeham, now newly appointed Surveyor of the King's Works, supervised the rebuilding of the Jewel House, on the south side of the White Tower, and saw to the strengthening of the roof of the White Tower, which had been damaged by the weight of heavy guns trained on the City and on the river. In 1536, Nedeham together with the Master of the Ordnance and his staff inspected the 'long howse of Ordnance' north of the White Tower and discovered it to be in a perilous state and ready to fall. They recommended that a new building should be constructed, but it was not until 1545 that funds were finally allocated. During the next two years, and at a cost of £2894, a new building was erected 'wherein all the Kinges majestie's store and provicon of artillerie Ordnance and other Municons' could be kept.

The new building can be seen as an extensive range against the inner curtain wall north of the White Tower on the 1597 survey (see **36**). To the west, on ground immediately behind the Chapel of St Peter, stood a substantial building,

38 *The Queen's House and its surroundings in 1720* (Royal Armouries).

part of which still survives. The remains include the lower stonework of the east elevation and two spacious brick-lined vaults which now form an amenity to the chapel; a third vault, now the crypt of the chapel, may also be associated. The origins of the building are not known, though the form of the two large doorways in the wall (one leading into the vaults, the other into the ground floor) suggest a late medieval or early Tudor date. It is possible that the building functioned as the Ordnance 'paiehouse' or Treasury House (first mentioned early in the reign of Elizabeth) before becoming the Ordnance administrative office by the time of the Restoration.

In 1540, after many requests and complaints, the Lieutenant of the Tower, Sir Edmund Walsingham, finally obtained funds from the Chamber to reconstruct his lodgings – the former Constable's house of Edward III's reign, occupying a position in the south-west corner of the Inner Ward. The present Queen's House, incorporating vestiges of the medieval house, dates substantially from this time and represents the most important Tudor building still to be found in the castle (**38**). Now the official residence of the Governor, this L-shaped timber-framed structure rests on the curtain walls behind it and exhibits four gabled bays in each range. Externally the building shows much of its original timber framing (including

39 *Artist's impressions of the great kitchen in the Queen's House during the middle of the sixteenth century.* Left *shows the fireplace in the east wall;* right *a suggested chamber at mezzanine level against the west wall* (Terry Ball).

ogee curved braces), except where masked by later accretions, notably on the ground floor. Internally, the rooms have undergone various alterations and refurbishments, particularly during the late seventeenth and early eighteenth centuries. The east–west wing appears to have contained the grandest rooms, including a fine first-floor hall in the penultimate western bay with a great first-floor kitchen in the most easterly, both open to the roof (**39**). The former must have been rather old fashioned by the architectural standards of the day, and this has led to suggestions that it may have formed part of the earlier house, though this has not been proved. Many of the roof timbers were removed in 1608 when a mezzanine floor was inserted (see below, p. 61) and the exact form of the original structure was only clearly understood

in 1979 when one of the missing tie-beams was found, reused as a window lintel in the south wall.

The Mint

The most significant archaeological evidence for the early Tudor Mint to be found at the Tower in recent years comes from Legge's Mount. Here, during the modernization of Warders' lodgings in 1976 a number of brick footings were encountered which, when excavated, were found to belong to a building associated with the Tudor Mint (**40**). The building had been constructed against the inner face of Legge's Mount while it functioned as an open bastion. The remains comprised the lower part of a vaulted cellar, containing a well, with an adjoining quadrant room to the north. Within the latter was the remains of a furnace, incorporating two key-shaped hearths and attached ash pit; the furnace was linked to the cellar by means of a culvert, possibly intended as an air duct; all were constructed in brick.

A range of metalworking finds, largely recovered from the ash pit, included about

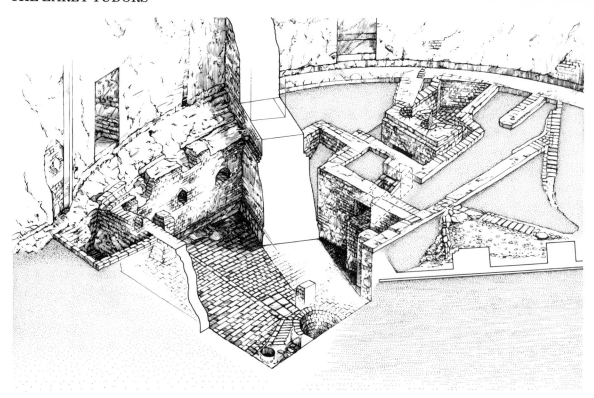

40 *Cut-away illustration of the remains of the Tudor Mint building excavated in Legge's Mount, 1976* (Peter Dunn).

twenty crucibles used for melting copper or one of its alloys (**colour plate 8**). Most were 15–20 cm (6–8 in) high, though some were smaller, with thinner walls, down to about 5 cm (2 in) high. Evidence for the working of precious metals was provided by a number of small cupels made from bone ash. These items, only 3 cm (*c.*1¼ in) in diameter, were used to test the purity of silver. This was achieved by adding a weighed sample of silver to a pool of molten lead on the cupel. As the cupel was heated, the lead oxide that was produced dissolved any base metal before being absorbed by the cupel, leaving a droplet of purified silver behind.

A further group of finds was formed by globular pottery flasks with long thin necks which were probably used to distil nitric acid employed to dissolve out silver from gold-silver alloys. All the vessels, and indeed the nature of the excavated furnace, indicate that the Legge's Mount building was connected with assaying, the process of testing the proportions of metals in alloys. In order to determine more precisely when these operations had been carried out, a relatively new method of dating called archaeomagnetic dating was employed. This involved calculating the direction of the earth's magnetic field when the furnace was last fired. When the data was compared with results from other dated sites, it was possible to calculate that the furnace had probably been heated for the last time between 1530 and 1560.

9

The later Tudors and early Stuarts

Under Elizabeth I the most substantial structural additions to the Tower were associated with the Mint and the need to reorganize the currency after the debasements of Henry VIII's last years. In 1560–2 £2853 0s 9¾d was spent on the Upper Mint, evidently a brick and timber building constructed at the southern end of the Outer Ward near the Salt Tower. At the same time, a new refining house was constructed in 'Coldharbour' the heart of the old palace south of the White Tower. In 1566 further work was carried out on 'the Blauching house and other places in the Mynt' and, in 1585–6, a new mint office was erected, probably that which can be seen against the outer curtain wall north of the Byward Tower on William Allingham's survey of the Mint, dated 1701.

Under James I the first improvement carried out was the construction in 1603–5 of a new floor in the White Tower to accommodate a 'powder house'. It is possible that this work refers to the introduction of the existing uppermost floor, but the association remains to be proved. During 1604–5 the lions' quarters within the barbican at the western entrance were renewed with two-storey dens fitted with stone openings and 'drawing doors' or traps worked with ropes and pulleys (**41**). At the same time a new platform was erected, from which the king could view the animals.

With the arrival of Sir William Waad as Lieutenant of the Tower in 1605 (an office he held for eight years) there was a bustle of activity associated with improvements to prisoners' lodgings. One of the most famous prisoners at this time was Sir Walter Ralegh who had entered the Tower in July 1603. During 1605–6, Ralegh's accommodation in the Bloody Tower was increased by dividing the gatehouse horizontally with a mezzanine floor. Of this addition, only a small lobby to the south (which probably functioned as a closet behind the bedchamber) survives, the remainder was recreated in 1974 on the evidence of the joist holes found in the walls. In order to allow better light, two new windows were provided; that in the west wall lighting the ground floor survives with its iron bars and 'locketts' (saddle bars) still in place, that in the north wall of the upper storey was renewed in the late nineteenth century, but can be identified on early photographs.

In 1607 Waad increased his own accommodation at the Queen's House by creating the so-called Council Chamber. This he achieved by inserting a floor into the great hall while at the same time removing some of the roof timbers; the principal light source for the new chamber was provided by a 'fayre Baye windowe' formed in the south wall (and now replaced by a modern arrangement). In the same room, on 9 October 1608, he erected a marble monument celebrating the thwarting of the gunpowder plot which still exists in the west wall. Also in 1608 he built a chamber over the thirteenth-century cross wall that extended from the Bell Tower towards the Byward Tower and in the following year converted a 'Rude chamber by the great chamber' into one of the most comfortable chambers in his lodgings. The rude chamber, which was supported by posts, was probably located to the east of the Council Chamber where it jettied into the ground-floor kitchen (see **39**). Part of the conversion involved extending the floor of the chamber fully over the kitchen to create the arrangement that exists today.

41 *A drawing of the inside of the Lion Tower in 1779 showing its two-tier cages* (Royal Armouries).

One of the few new buildings to be erected during the reign of James I was a two-storeyed house for the Tower parson (see **60**). Built in 1616–17, it was of timber construction 8.2 by 5m (27 by 16 ft) and probably stood against the rear of the inner curtain wall to the west end of the Chapel of St Peter, on the site of the present chaplain's house. Though seemingly undocumented, the attractive brick houses against the curtain wall immediately north of the Queen's House (Nos. 4 and 5 Tower Green) would also appear to date from this time, or perhaps a little later. They certainly were in existence by the time of the Restoration, and by the 1680s were appropriated by the Lieutenant, possibly functioning as lodgings for his secretary or other servants.

In 1632–3 considerable efforts were made to improve the condition of the Wharf, with whole sections being taken down and rebuilt. At the same time camp-shedding was installed and timber fenders fitted to reduce the damage caused by ships while mooring. Later, in 1634–5, 156 piles were sunk for the foundation

of an 'apron' at the water-gate. The apron was designed to stop vessels from getting stuck in the mud at low tide. Chalk was rammed into the groundwork, but otherwise the device was entirely carpenters' work. Part of the structure, which was 4.1m (13 ft 6 ins) wide and extended beneath Traitors' Bridge to the south of the river entrance, was revealed by excavation in 1973–4 (**42**).

By June 1636 a decision had been taken to begin large-scale repairs within the castle. The White Tower attracted the largest expenditure, and here in 1637–8 much of the decayed ashlar in the angles of the building, the arches over the windows, the turrets and battlements, was replaced in Portland stone, thus beginning a process that by the eighteenth century gave the tower an appearance which it retains to this day.

Throughout the later Tudor and early Stuart periods little effort was made to modernize the Tower's defences. In contrast with other military sites at this time no bastions were added to the outer wall to provide covering fire and none of the tall medieval towers was cut down to serve as gun emplacements. Instead wooden gun platforms were installed over existing roofs. An estimate for repairing platforms in

42 *Remains of apron constructed beneath St Thomas's Tower in 1634–5; seen here during excavations in 1974* (Nicolette Hallet).

1564 identifies devices on the four sides of the White Tower, Devereux and Flint towers, St Thomas's Tower and two locations in the Mint.

Around the moat and the Bulwark at the western entrance, encroachments had so weakened the defences that by the beginning of the seventeenth century they were judged to be of little military value. Repeated calls to remove the offending buildings and to cleanse the silted moat produced no results until after the Restoration and the intervention of the Great Fire of 1666 (see below, p. 75).

One notable, though seemingly undocumented, piece of work which can be attributed to this period, was the remodelling of Legge's Mount on the north-west corner of the Outer Ward. During the investigations carried out here in 1976, it was found that the ground-floor brickwork of the rear and flank walls had probably been constructed during the second quarter of the seventeenth century, or perhaps during the Civil War. The whole had been covered with a brick bomb vault which was removed during the heightening of the building in 1682–3. The work necessitated demolition of much of the Tudor assay building that stood within the bastion though the cellar continued in use with some form of replacement timber roof supported on brick piers. Brass Mount on the opposing north-east corner had been, as the 1597 survey indicates, enclosed at an earlier date. Here, however, no attempt was made to create internal accommodation, rather the core of the bastion was infilled with earth to cushion cannon shot and paved over to provide a platform for mounting guns (evidently heavy brass pieces, hence its name).

10

The later Stuarts

The building history of the Tower under the later Stuarts was dominated by the Office of Ordnance. In the wake of the Restoration the Office assumed sole responsibility for the defences and within the walls began to assert control over larger and larger areas. This expansion was accompanied by major building campaigns, which by 1700 had caused the overall plan of the fortress to change quite dramatically.

The reconstruction of the palace ward
The programme of reconstruction effectively began three years after the Restoration in the eastern confines of the old palace complex. A royal warrant dated 17 January 1663 recited:

> Whereas wee have received information of the great want of convenient Roomes in the storehouses belonging to the Office of our ordnance within our Tower of London . . . Our will and pleasure is that the void peece of ground . . . commonly knowne or called by the name of the wardrobe Garden bee assigned . . . toward the erecting and building of a Storehouse for laying up our said Armes and provisions.

During February and March the first of several imprests of money were made to John Scott, carpenter, and Thomas Norfolk, bricklayer. In May 'Traitors bridge Gate' was ordered to be cleared to receive building materials and in July the paving of a road to the new building and a court before it, was ordered. A year later the principal bills were settled at a cost of just over £4000 and by the autumn 2232 yards of 'Broad Bullrush Matts' had been laid in the 'small Gun Office Roome', racking installed and three furbishers paid for 'oyleing ffixinge and

cleaneing the Arms' that were transferred into the building from the White Tower. A few weeks later, on 8 November, Samuel Pepys surveyed the Tower storehouses in the company of the King and various officials and considered that with the addition of the new great storehouse they were 'a noble sight'.

The new storehouse so expeditiously erected and fitted out was in fact the present New Armouries Building which stands against the rear of the curtain between the Broad Arrow and Salt towers (**43**). It now represents the only surviving Ordnance store at the Tower and probably the oldest surviving Ordnance building in the country. Constructed of red brick and half H-shaped in plan, it comprises two floors and a double attic (**44**).

The next phase of work was carried out to the west of the new storehouse in the heart of the old palace, then loosely referred to as 'Cold-harbour'. This was partly necessitated by the threat that some of the old buildings posed to the powder magazine within the White Tower. As early as March 1661 a committee of peers had recommended the creation of a safety corridor 20 ft wide around the tower, but little or no action appears to have been taken. On 5 March 1666, another committee was instructed to consider where military stores, especially stores of powder, could be lodged with safety and convenience. Furthermore, they were required to find a new route for transporting stores into the fortress with greater ease. In its report the committee argued that the existing facilities for proving powder should be moved from the courtyard within the former medieval wardrobe building annexed to the east side of the White Tower, to a new site on the Wharf. From here a new passage was to be created to

1 A late fifteenth-century manuscript illustration showing Charles Duke of Orleans in the White Tower. Note St Thomas's Tower in the foreground and the palace buildings, including the hall and the two chamber blocks either side, behind and to the right *(British Library)*.

WESTERN ENTRANCE OF THE TOWER OF LONDON C.1400

4 Watercolour of the Beauchamp Tower and its surroundings by Charles Tomkins in 1801, looking east *(Guildhall Library)*.

2 *(Above left)* Artist's impression of the riverside defences during the reign of Henry III, showing the Wakefield Tower and water entrances, with the Bell Tower to the far left *(Terry Ball)*.

3 *(Below left)* Artist's impression of the Western Entrance in *c.*1400 *(Terry Ball)*.

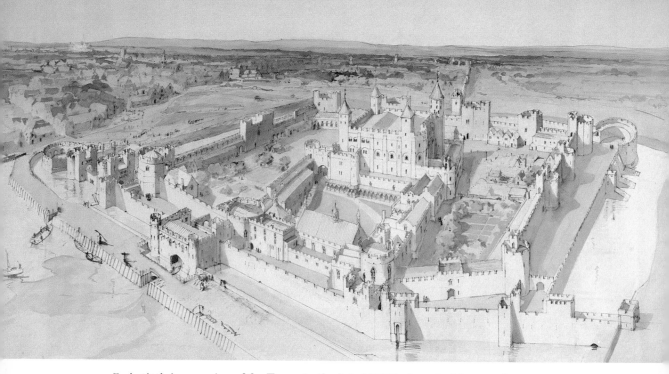

5 Artist's impression of the Tower in the late Middle Ages looking north-west *(Terry Ball)*.

6 Artist's impression of the Tower in the middle of the sixteenth century looking south-east *(Terry Ball)*.

7 Detail of St Michael from the late fourteenth-century mural painting in the
Byward Tower *(Photo: Damian Gillie)*.

8 *(Above)* Some of the Tudor metalworking vessels recovered from the excavation of the Mint building in Legge's Mount, 1976 *(Photo: English Heritage)*.

10 *(Right)* Elevation of the Western Entrance in 1845, showing the Spur Guard to the left of the Middle Tower and the Porter's lodgings to the right *(Public Record Office)*.

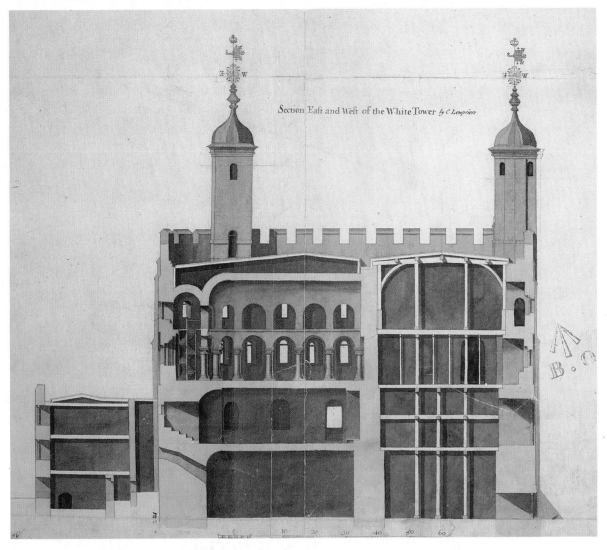

9 *(Above)* East-west section through the White Tower by Clement Lemprière, 1729 *(Public Record Office)*.

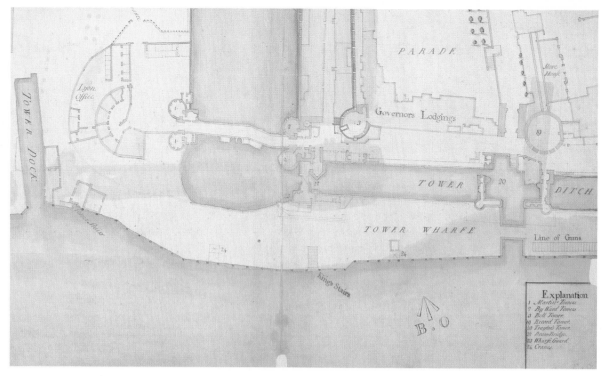

11 Plan of the south-west corner of the Tower in 1726 *(Public Record Office)*.

12 Artist's impression of the Tower as it appears today from the south-east *(Terry Ball)*.

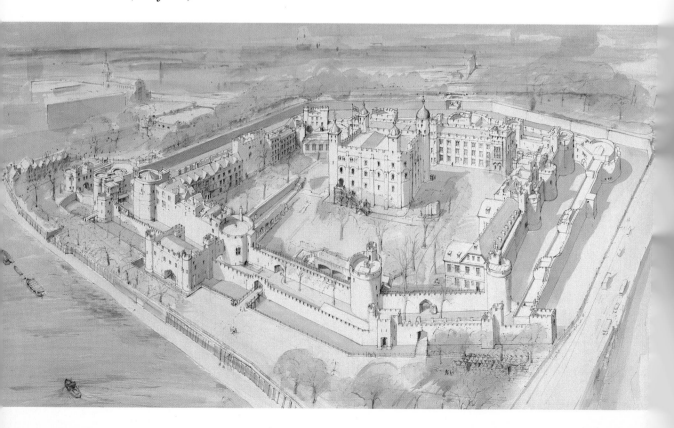

43 *The New Armouries Building* (right) *and Old Hospital Block looking north-east* (Historic Royal Palaces Agency).

allow the powder to be transported directly to the White Tower. The new route would involve the construction of a bridge over the moat and the breaching of the inner and outer curtain walls; various old buildings close to the White Tower, including the only part of the palace still maintained for royal use, would have to be demolished. If all of this was done, and other Ordnance stores 'lodged there abouts altogether' the committee estimated that the cost of transporting supplies to the Tower could be significantly reduced, while the time taken to supply the fleet would be reduced from more than twenty to just four days.

In November 1666 the Ordnance was authorized to implement the proposals, an event that heralded the start of nearly ten years of continuous building work that was to transform the old palace ward beyond recognition. In addition to the measures just described, two further passages, both presumably linked to the planned route from the Wharf, were also ordered to be made. One, which was to run to the proof yard on the east side of the White Tower, involved demolition of part of the old

Jewel House, the other, directed to the new storehouse, passed through an old hall that formed part of the Queen's Lodgings between the Lanthorn and Wardrobe towers. To safeguard the powder magazine in the White Tower it was ordered that all the chimneys belonging to the old buildings adjoining the south side of the keep, as well as those associated with the Coldharbour Gate, should be demolished and no manner of replacement permitted.

Work on the committee's proposals began almost immediately and by June the following year the new drawbridge, whose position corresponded to that of the present Middle Drawbridge, was in place. Amidst this activity another royal warrant appeared on 22 April 1667 which read:

> Wee have thought fitt suitable to those our first Intentions and directions . . . that forthwith you give Order for the demollishing altering and new Building all that grownde and old buildings in the Tower called Cold Harbour.

Within the area the Ordnance was to erect such new storehouses and buildings as were considered necessary for the king's service.

On 3 April 1668 the commissioners appointed to oversee the works presented a report to the

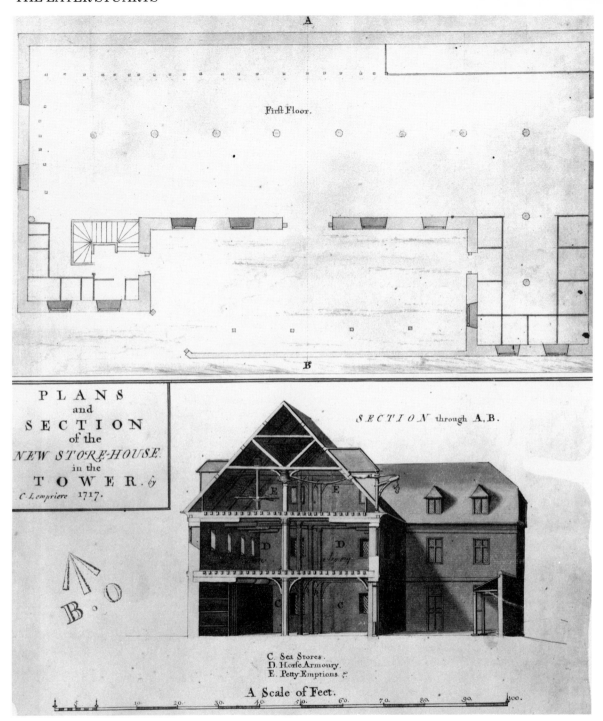

44 *Plan and section of the New Armouries Building by Clement Lemprière in 1717. The interior timber frame includes an interesting series of octagonal columns with carved bases.* *On the ground floor these are accompanied by ceiling braces with applied mouldings to imitate capitals* (Public Record Office).

Privy Council outlining 12 further measures deemed necessary to safeguard the powder magazine in the White Tower. These included the vacation and boarding up of all the old buildings on the south and west sides of the tower, including the Coldharbour Gate, the residual royal lodgings, the remains of the Jewel House and various buildings occupied by Yeoman Warders and others. Furthermore, the idea of forming a safety corridor around the White Tower was resurrected so that the building could 'stand clear from any Person coming near'.

The implementation of the latest proposals seems to have begun with Sir Gilbert Talbot, Master and Treasurer of the King's Jewels, being requested by the Ordnance to remove the Regalia from the Jewel House to allow a speedy demolition of the building. Talbot complained that there was no other place in the Tower to house the jewels and as a consequence the Ordnance was obliged to convert the 'Irish Tower' (i.e. Martin Tower) into a new depository. The Crown Jewels were to be housed on the ground floor with the Keeper's apartment above – the existing mezzanine floor in the upper chamber evidently dates from this time. The operation must have been nearing completion by June 1669, when the Jewel Keeper, Talbot Edwards, was ordered to leave his house in Coldharbour.

By now work on the corridor around the White Tower was underway with hundreds of stakes, 2.75m (9 ft) long, being employed in a palisade. By the beginning of 1670 the Ordnance builders had also built three new houses in the Outer Ward, some 30m (100 ft) north of the Develin Tower, for Yeoman Warders whose houses in Coldharbour had been confiscated. Elsewhere, workmen were pulling down the 'long powder house' which had been formed out of the Tudor Wardrobe situated between the Broad Arrow and Wardrobe towers in 1650.

In July 1670 the first of several bills was settled for the construction of a new storehouse in Coldharbour. A modest, brick-built structure of two storeys, this can almost certainly be identified as the 'Little Storehouse' shown on the 1688 survey against the curtain wall south of the site of the Coldharbour Gate (**45**). The building appears to have been nearly finished by the end of 1671 and between March and April the following year the carpenter was 'fitting up the Traine of Artilery' within.

During 1672–3 the builders were busy preparing a new administrative office for the Ordnance in Coldharbour to replace their old one behind the Chapel of St Peter ad Vincula. The T-shaped building stood immediately north of the Lanthorn Tower and to the east of the former medieval great hall, which now acted as the largest Ordnance storehouse in Coldharbour. The office was, in fact, not so much a new building, but more the adaptation of an old one, since the core of the structure comprised part of the old Queen's Lodgings. An account with the joiner lists rooms assigned to three senior offices of the Board and four named clerks. In addition there was a 'Clerkes Room', a 'Great Roome' (presumably the 'Board Room' shown on later eighteenth-century surveys) with an 'Anteroome' attached. The Great Room and the Anteroom were fitted with three sash windows each (a device not long introduced into England so that it is perhaps not surprising that they were especially noted in the account); presumably the other rooms were lighted by more conventional casements. Most of the rooms were wainscotted and all provided with combinations of desks, tables, cupboards, presses, shelves and screens.

The building was evidently ready for occupation by the end of September 1673, when the officers and clerks were instructed to 'remove all their Bookes, papers and writeings to the new Office . . . without ffayle'. Perhaps as an amenity for the new office a clock turret was constructed in 1673–4 on top of the Wardrobe Tower at the south-east corner of the White Tower. The structure was faced with free-stone ashlar, was battlemented and capped with a cupola. It housed an extraordinary clock supplied by Thomas Tompion for £45 and was also furnished with sundials that were painted and gilded. The turret proved to be a short-lived affair, being demolished in 1715 after the Board was advised that it was too narrow to carry the cupola and therefore in danger of falling.

With their office finished the Ordnance embarked upon the next stage of the programme – the demolition of all the remaining old buildings contiguous to the south side of the White Tower. On 10 March 1674, in a probable reference to the twelfth-century forebuilding, the Surveyor General, Sir Jonas More, was instructed to prepare a contract for 'pullinge downe the Tower against the White Tower'. On

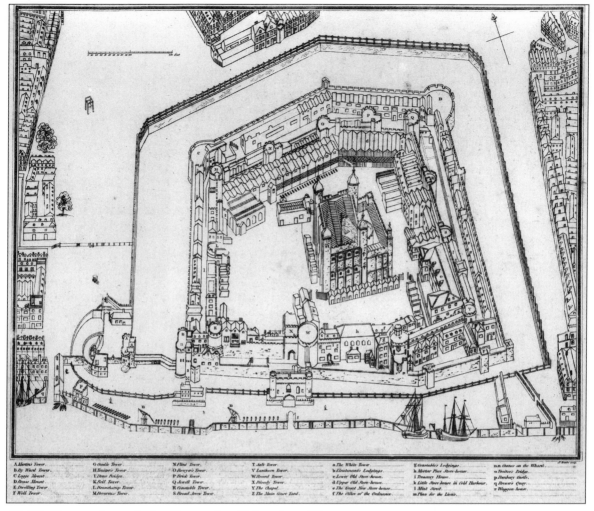

45 *Bird's-eye-view of the Tower by Holcroft Blood, 1688* (Royal Armouries).

24 March a great screw was ordered on to the site to help dismantle the ruinous walls. The operation appears to have been completed by August when several heaps of stone were ordered off the site so that work on the palisade around the White Tower could be concluded (see **58**). During demolition considerable interest was generated when, on 17 July, the remains of two small children were discovered, apparently below the stairs leading from the forebuilding to the Chapel in the White Tower. The bones were identified as belonging to the 'Little Princes in the Tower' and on the instructions of Charles II reburied in Westminster Abbey.

There now remained only one major task to complete the reconstruction of the palace ward – the removal of the Coldharbour Gate, Henry III's entrance into the ward by the south-west corner of the White Tower. On 16 September 1675 the lead over the gatehouse was ordered to be removed and delivered to Greenwich to cover the roof of the Royal Observatory, then under construction. On 18 November, a team of labourers was contracted to demolish the gate, a task completed before July the following year, when an estimate to complete the palisade around the White Tower was ordered to be prepared. With the great tower now free of accretions for the first time in nearly four hundred years a contract was signed with the Ordnance mason on 1 August 1676 for repairing the recently exposed elevations and for constructing a new staircase of 25 steps against the south face to provide access to the Record Office in the Chapel on the first floor.

In addition to the new storage accommodation in Coldharbour, the Ordnance continued to repair and maintain its existing stores on the

46 *(Above) Late seventeenth-century arms of the Board of Ordnance now mounted on the south wall of the New Armouries Building (Royal Armouries).*

hill north of the White Tower and in the White Tower itself. In January 1669 a contract for new weather vanes to be installed on the turrets of the White Tower was drawn up. In their bill dated 7 June that year, Ralp Greatorix and William Partridge were paid £200 for '4 ffanes and Crownes with a strong crosse of iron with the fower Letters E.W.N.S. under each ffane with a convenient counter poize handlike holding a ball and crosse'. The weather vanes, which were painted 'lead' colour with their details gilded, still survive, though the counterbalances were replaced with large arrows sometime towards the end of the eighteenth century (**48**).

The continuing demand for storage facilities saw long rows of timber sheds erected in 1685–6 against the palisade on the east, west and south sides of the White Tower and down the east side of Coldharbour, opposite the New Armouries Building (see **45**). Some 4.25m

47 *(Below) Engraving of the Tower from the river, c.1710 (Guildhall Library).*

48 *One of the four weather vanes mounted on the turrets of the White Tower in 1669* (Royal Armouries).

(14 ft) wide and 2.75m (9 ft) high, most appear to have been intended for the reception of small arms, though those on the south side of the White Tower were described as sheds for wagons.

The building of the Grand Storehouse
In January 1687 George Legge, the Master General of the Ordnance, was advised of the 'crazy condition' of the old storehouses to the north of the White Tower and of the inadequate protection they provided for the stores lodged within. After a year's deliberation a draft and estimate for a single new storehouse was prepared and on 1 March 1688 Legge gave instruc-

tions for work to proceed. The building was to be the most impressive structure ever built by the Ordnance at the Tower and was, until the end of its life in 1841, known as the Grand Storehouse.

In advance of building work, a mass of stores and other material needed to be removed from the various old buildings and lodged elsewhere. Among the items were two displays of historic armour known as the Line of Kings and the Spanish Armour. The former comprised a series of figures representing the Kings of England; they appeared on horseback wearing what was claimed to have been their personal property. The second collection, the Spanish Armour, consisted of various trophies said to have been captured from the Armada of 1588. In May 1688 the Ordnance carpenter was paid for 'fitting up a Roome in Cold harbour . . . for placing the Spanish Armoury' and for 'takeing downe the Wooden horses' and 'placeing them in the Scotch storehouse'. The new home for the Spanish Armoury was in fact the upper floor of the storehouse erected in 1670–1 against the curtain wall north of the Wakefield Tower, while that for the Line of Kings was the eastern room on the first floor of the White Tower, though this was only a temporary measure before the collection found a permanent home in the New Armouries Building.

While the contents of the old storehouses were being moved the Ordnance pressed ahead with arrangements for the construction of the new building. On 29 March 1688 a contract was signed with Thomas and John Fitch for the demolition of the old buildings and the construction of the new one. On 5 April a certain Robert Baker was appointed overseer of works. Work must have commenced almost immediately since Baker began to draw his fee four days later and continued to do so until the end of 1691 when he was awarded a gratuity for his service at the 'storehouse being now finish'd'.

The Grand Storehouse was a building of some architectural pretension. It was nearly 110m (360 ft) long, 18m (60 ft) wide and comprised two storeys and attic below a steeply pitched, lead-covered roof (**49**). The main body of the building was constructed of brick with Portland stone employed in the frontispiece and dressings. The whole was crowned by a great pediment containing martial arms (**50**) carved by John Young – the only element of the building still surviving. Finally, midway along

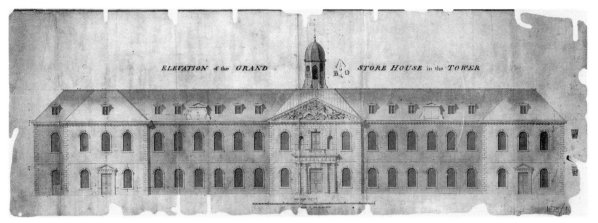

49 *Mid eighteenth-century elevation of the Grand Storehouse* (Public Record Office).

the rear (north) elevation was a large stair turret. This in fact contained two staircases; one provided access to the roof storey or rag loft, the other, a more spacious arrangement known as the Grand Staircase, was reserved for members of the royal family, or any of the nobility, visiting the displays housed on the first floor (see **51**).

Some writers have attributed the design of the Grand Storehouse to Sir Christopher Wren or the principal building contractor Sir Thomas Fitch. However, there is no evidence in the official papers to suppose that the design emanated from outside the Ordnance Office. There is clear evidence for amendments to the building during construction since the principal bill is supplemented by a second for 'over worke not mentioned in the Contract'. The frontispiece, ornate dormer windows and imposing octagonal cupola are among the items shown to be additional to the original draft. Also mentioned is the cutting out of the cyphers of James II from the keystones of the lower windows – a reminder that the building campaign spanned the upheavals of November 1688. In fact, the political changes that accompanied the 'Glorious Revolution' might have provided the impetus to redefine the role of the Grand Storehouse. No longer was it to be regarded solely as a depository for stores, instead the entire first floor was to be given over to remarkable displays of figures and designs, largely composed of weapons, known as the Small Armoury. It is quite possible that these tableaux and the architectural embellishment of the building, as

represented in the 'over worke', were conceived as part of a scheme to create a military showpiece at the Tower by the Protestant administration that replaced that of the deposed king, James II. As time went by, the Grand Storehouse became more and more a museum of Britain's martial might and the ground floor, which housed the train of artillery, was gradually given over to a display of guns and trophies captured from battlefields around the world.

Concerning the total cost of construction, the final bills settled with the widow of Sir Thomas Fitch and his brother John amounted to £13,942 12s 3d. In addition, over £500 was spent on items not included in the main contract. This included £155 to John Young for carving the great arms for the pediment and £49 18s 0d to Robert Bird for making and gilding a 'Copper faine, scrolles and flower pot' and 'Globe' to surmount the cupola.

According to the eighteenth-century historian William Maitland, the completion of the Grand Storehouse was marked by a magnificent banquet on the first floor, at which King William and Queen Mary were waited on by the warranted workmen and labourers wearing white gloves and aprons, the badges of freemasonry. Presumably this would have occurred sometime in early 1692, though no further documentary reference is known.

The Small Armoury in the Grand Storehouse

During January 1696, the Ordnance Board issued orders for 'fitting up the middle Roome of the great Storehouse . . . for an Armoury of small Guns'. The work was carried out under the direction of one John Harris of Eton; a

50 *The great martial arms carved by John Young in 1691 for the pediment of the Grand Storehouse. Now on display in the New Armouries Building* (photo: Jeremy Hall, Royal Armouries).

51 *Plan of the Small Armoury in the Grand Storehouse. Re-drawn from a survey of 1718 by Lewis Petit now in the Public Record Office* (English Heritage).

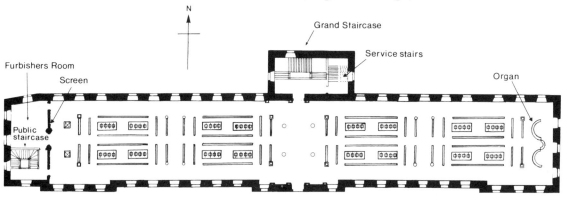

DISPLAY FEATURES

52 *Decorative screen erected at the west end of the Small Armoury in 1696. Drawing by Lewis Petit, 1718* (Public Record Office).

gunsmith by trade, he is known to have contrived designs with obsolete weapons to decorate the walls of the guard chambers at Hampton Court, Windsor Castle and St James's Palace. Harris was assisted at the Tower by the master carpenter, Henry Haywood, and the master carver, Nicholas Allcock, who received £2091 8s 0d and £611 2s 3d respectively for their work.

Access to the Small Armoury, for the visiting public, was via a staircase at the west end of the building (**51**). Having ascended to the first floor visitors passed through a low screen (**52**). Beyond lay the full array of Harris's exuberant tableaux, a sight which, according to Maitland 'no one ever beheld without Astonishment . . . not to be matched perhaps in the world'. The north and south walls were each adorned with eight pilasters composed of pikes 5m (16 ft) long, bearing capitals of pistols set in the Corinthian order. Between them Harris arranged his most spectacular creations. These included moons and fans composed of bayonets and pistols arranged around an imitation target of bayonet blades and another set in carved scallop shells decorated with 'ornaments of pearls and Currell with drops of Shells at the Ends'. The 'Waves of the Sea' were reproduced in bayonets and brass blunderbusses with capitals of pistols over them. There was a representation of the rising sun, irradiated with rays of

pistols, as well as a pair of folding ceremonial gates within an arch made of halberds and horsemen's carbines and a battery of guns in swords and pistols. The 'Back Bones of a Whale' were made of carbines and, perhaps Harris's finest creation, Medusa's Head 'commonly caled the Witch of Endor' set within three regular ellipses of pistols. The centre of the device was of carved work, described in Allcock's account as a 'Target carved with Medusass head, snakes & Ornaments of foldage'. Among other decorative items provided by Allcock to adorn the walls was the figure of Jupiter riding 'a fiery Chariot drawn by Eagles, as if in the Clouds, holding a Thunder-bolt in his left Hand, and over his Head a Rainbow'.

At the eastern extremity of the room stood the figure of a great organ, ten ranges high, its large pipes made out of brass blunderbusses, its smaller ones by upwards of two thousand pairs of pistols. The organ was flanked by a 'fiery serpent' and a 'seven-headed Monster'. For the former Allcock provided 'A Large Snakes head . . . 2 foot 6 inch by 2 foot . . . Carved with flames of fire great Fines & other ornaments' and a 'Snakes Tayl 6 foot 6 inch long, 15 inch broad . . . Carved with festoons of shells pearls and Gudring'. The body was composed of pistols and appeared to wind round. The hydra was made of carved heads and wings artificially joined with links of pistols. Completing the display at the east end of the room, standing in the corners below semi-circles of pistols, were two suits of armour attributed to Henry V and Henry VI.

53 *Design for the decoration of the south wall of the King's Guard Chamber at Windsor Castle, c.1680. The decoration of this room with large numbers of weapons and other military items was one of the first of its kind in England and therefore pre-dates the work of John Harris during the 1690s and early years of the eighteenth century* (Royal Armouries).

In the centre of the room, embellishing the route from the Grand Staircase to the balcony over the main entrance, stood four great columns some 7m (22 ft) high. These were largely the work of the master carpenter Haywood who decorated them with circular twisted elm mouldings to which he applied 900 pins for hanging pistols. Allcock provided Corinthian capitals, eight dragon faces and carved *in situ* the twisted mouldings with leaves, flowers and berries. To the underside of the ceiling, between the columns, he added a large pendant in the form of a falling star.

At the west end of the room Harris created two pyramids of pistols capped with carved wooden heads. These were arranged on eight circular ornaments that stood on wooden pedestals 1.5m (5 ft) high. Finally, down the centre of the room was a series of large gun racks interspersed with eight square and eight

circular columns of pikes and pistols capped with carved Corinthian capitals. Surveys dating from the middle of the eighteenth century indicate that the whole was arranged around 16 large chests which were said to contain 1200 muskets each.

By any standard the Small Armoury was a remarkable affair. In general terms, many of the displays can be seen as an extension of the tradition of decorating guard chambers in the royal palaces (**53**) with fanciful designs such as still can be seen at Hampton Court, though the use of free-standing devices, like the seven-headed monster, evidently represented an innovation. The source of Harris's inspiration is obscure, and no documentary reference has been found to show whether any other individuals within, or without, the Ordnance were concerned with the concept and its execution. Looking at the layout, the free-standing and engaged columns seem to have provided an architectural framework for the various displays, with the four great pillars forming a crossing in the centre of the room. Perhaps the aisled plan mirrored that of a church – a distinct possibility when the presence of the great organ at the east end of the room is taken into account. By comparison, no theme seems to have pervaded the designs and figures, representing as they did such diverse subjects as the head of the mythological Medusa and the backbone of a whale. No illustration of the tableaux have so far come to light and the loss of this fabulous collection by fire in 1841 must be counted as one of the greatest single tragedies to have beset the Tower.

The waterworks

Fire was a constant threat to the Tower and its establishments. Given the physical pre-dominance of the Ordnance within the walls at this time it is perhaps not surprising that the Office was responsible for maintaining the castle's water supply. In fact the Ordnance had been preoccupied with this vital task since at least the 1620s when a certain John Palmer was paid for 'pomping of water in the water-works at the Tower to serve the Lieutenents howse and the houses belonging to the Officers of the Ordnance and other the inhabitants [of] his Majesties servants and to have water alwaies in redines to prevent the danger of fire'. The waterworks at this date presum-ably occupied the same site as they did at the time of the Restoration – that is to say the east side of the basin below St Thomas's Tower. From here water was pumped into lead cisterns on top of the White Tower before being con-veyed to all parts of the fortress.

In 1663 the Office carpenter repaired the waterworks and supplied 160 'coggs for the Wheel' while the founder provided four new handles. By the end of 1675, however, the Board decided that an entire new engine was needed. In his bill dated 6 October 1676, Issac Thompson, engineer, was paid £42 for the 'Water Engine by him made and provided of brasse & iron for raiseinge the Water into the Cisterne above in the Tower' with, it was claimed, 'the strength of one man aboute twoe tuns of water in an howre'. The machine could evidently be powered by water currents or by a horse-driven treadmill.

Ordnance lodgings

According to their Instructions, Ordnance offic-ials were required to 'make their Ordinary Habitation and Aboad in the houses and Lodge-ings Assigned them in or neare the Tower'. Many lodgings were to be found against the rear of the curtain wall between the Martin and Broad Arrow towers, adjoining or near the Lanthorn Tower and in and about the Dever-eux Tower. Much of the work associated with these lodgings during the later Stuart era was concerned with general repair and refur-bishment. Relatively few new buildings were erected, the grandest being two great houses erected for the Surveyor and the Clerk of the Ordnance between 1699 and 1701 on the site of the present Fusiliers Museum, at a cost of over £4000 (**54**). Perhaps the only surviving exam-ple of domestic accommodation from this period is the building adjoining the south side of the Chaplain's house to the west of the Chapel of St Peter's (**55**). Now the residence of the Tower doctor and wrapped in an eighteenth-century brick skin, this is possibly a house built for one of the Ordnance clerks in 1686.

The fortifications and the garrison

So to the last major aspect of the Tower that concerned the Ordnance at this time – the fortifications. In an age when the development of military fortifications based on the bastioned system offered the only effective response to heavier and more powerful artillery, the old and obsolete medieval defences of the Tower presented a particular problem to the Ord-nance engineers.

In January 1664 the Privy Council set up a commission to ascertain, amongst other things, what encroachments had been made upon the Wharf, moat, walls and gates; to report on how the moat could be cleansed and enlarged; to examine defects in, and obstructions along, the walls; and to recommend where ordnance could best be planted to defend the Tower towards the land side. The commission was evidently slow to deliberate and no record of its final report appears to have survived. Whatever recommendations were made, it is very doubt-ful whether they were acted upon, since there is no record of expenditure on the defences at this time other than small sums for general maintenance.

The perennial problem of encroachments about the moat and western entrance was finally resolved in a somewhat dramatic fashion in September 1666, when the offending structures were summarily demolished to pre-vent the flames of the Great Fire from reaching the fortress. In the wake of the City's destruc-tion the whole question of the Tower's defences was considered again and between 20 and 24 November 1666, Sir Bernard de Gomme, the Ordnance Chief Engineer, was engaged in 'makeinge a draught of [the] Tower and

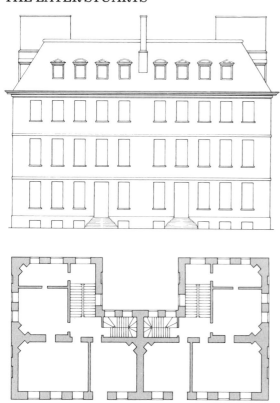

55 *Houses of the resident Chaplain* (right) *and Doctor of the Tower next to the Chapel of St Peter ad Vincula.* (Photo: Garry Kennard, Royal Armouries).

54 *Ground plan and elevation of the great houses built for the Surveyor and Clerk of the Ordnance in 1699–1701* (David Honour).

designe of fortifieinge the same'. A plan drawn by de Gomme at this time (**56**), shows that he proposed to replace much of the western entrance with a great ravelin, the moat was to be revetted on the three landward sides with a new wall, the old Postern Gate at the southern extremity of the City wall overlooking the moat was to be rebuilt, while a new wall and gate were envisaged at the eastern end of the Wharf. Evidently more radical solutions were considered, and a surviving draft, probably also by de Gomme, shows massive angular bastions to the outer wall (**57**).

Although plans for the introduction of a bastioned trace were never to leave the drawing board, some of de Gomme's other recommendations seem to have been acted upon. Demolition of the old Bulwark began in November 1668 and towards the end of 1670 the bricklayers were taking down the 'outward great gate', presumably the principal entrance

situated on the north-east corner of the enclosure (see **36**). During 1670 a new wall and gate were constructed in brick to the north of the Lion Tower. With regard to the moat, some of the long awaited improvements were carried out between July 1670 and December 1672 when the north and west banks were cut back and revetted with a substantial brick wall. The existing masonry, though much repaired, is of that date.

The accommodation of the garrison also received attention at this time, with plans for the first purposely designed soldiers' lodgings being prepared for a site in the Mint against the curtain wall between the Salt and Broad Arrow towers (**58**). On 27 May 1669 orders were placed with the Office bricklayer and carpenter to begin work. Comprised of two storeys and an attic, the 'Irish Barracks' as it became known, was essentially a timber-framed building with weather-boarded exterior. It was evidently ready for occupation by the end of the summer of 1670 when an account with the carpenter was settled for over £1000.

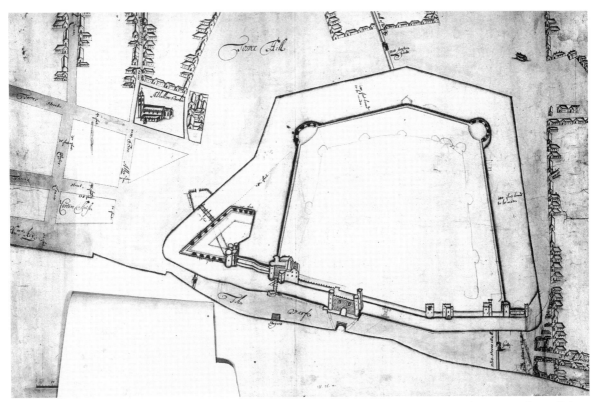

56 *A design for strengthening the defences of the Tower by Sir Bernard de Gomme, 1666 (Royal Armouries).*

Advised of 'diverse great Abuses & Encroachments' the Privy Council established a committee to examine the state and condition of the Tower in November 1679. The committee made a number of recommendations, most concerning the riverside defences and accommodation of the garrison. Consequently, in February 1680, contracts were signed with the bricklayers to enlarge the ramparts along the outer south curtain wall and to demolish the old medieval causeway leading from the Iron Gate to the Develin Tower so that 'the water of the Ditch may Runn round'. Further contracts were signed in March for taking down the Iron Gate and defensive wall at the east end of the Wharf and for building a new wall slightly farther to the west. Finally, the 'Old Sally porte' (i.e. Cradle Tower) was ordered to be walled up and about 35 yards of the remaining Bulwark near the Wharf taken down after the Board was informed that it was on the point of collapse.

Despite these measures the general condition of the Tower's defences and the facilities for the garrison continued to cause concern. On 2 December 1681, therefore, yet another committee was ordered to carry out an inspection and to make recommendations. The committee's findings were read before Council on 8 February 1682. The minute states that 'his Majesty taking the said Report into consideration was pleased to approve thereof, & did Order that it be'. During the next six years virtually all 32 articles contained in the report were acted upon. This represented a very considerable body of work; nothing on this scale had been attempted since the repairs ordered by Thomas Cromwell in 1532–3 and nothing so all-embracing has been witnessed since.

Against the outer curtain wall, at various locations along the landward defences, timber gun platforms were constructed, while on the north-west corner, Legge's Mount was raised some 6m (19 ft) to its present height to accommodate two tiers of guns – the existing brick gun-ports on the first floor date from this time. To the south a large gun platform was planted on St Thomas's Tower and two smaller devices over the twin towers of the Byward Tower.

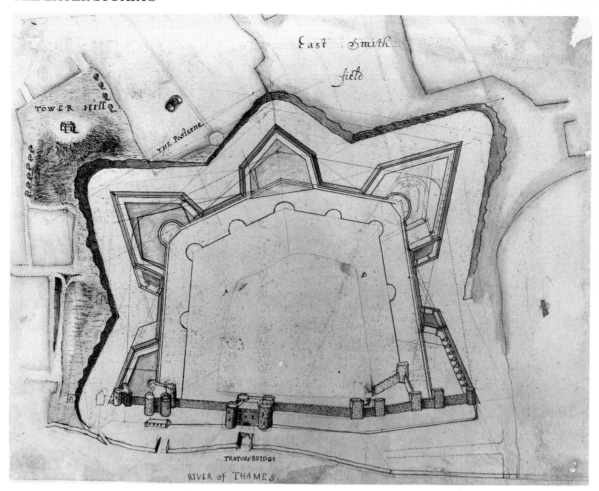

East Smith field

TOWER HILL

THE Posterne

TRATORS BRIDGE

RIVER of THAMES.

57 *A design for adding large artillery bastions to the outer landward defences of the Tower. Probably draughted by Sir Bernard de Gomme, c.1666 (Ashmolean Museum).*

Similar alterations were made to the mural towers along the three landward sides of the inner curtain wall. Communications between the towers were improved and two surviving sally ports punched through the curtain wall immediately west of the Martin Tower and midway between the Flint and Devereux towers.

Within the walls various coach-houses and stables were converted into accommodation for soldiers and gunners. Another barrack block was built in the Mint opposite the principal lodgings erected in 1669–70. Parts of Legge's Mount were equipped to receive two companies of guards while a third was quartered in the western half of St Thomas's Tower.

Within the Inner Ward a new parade ground was laid out to the north of the Queen's House on the site of the Lieutenant's garden and a bowling green, while the old main guard, located to the south-east of the Beauchamp Tower, was demolished and a new one constructed near the north-west corner of the White Tower. Finally, the retaining wall was continued down the east side of the moat while the board thoughtfully made provision for 'a Raile . . . to prevent peoples falling in'.

In 1688, with all the improvements implemented, the Ordnance engineer Holcroft Blood produced a series of drawings of the Tower. Among these is a curious bird's-eye-view which evidently took Blood four months to prepare, and which is described in his account as a 'Draught of the Tower Rais'd in Perspective upon the Ground' (see **45**).

Throughout the concluding Stuart period the defences were subject to little more than

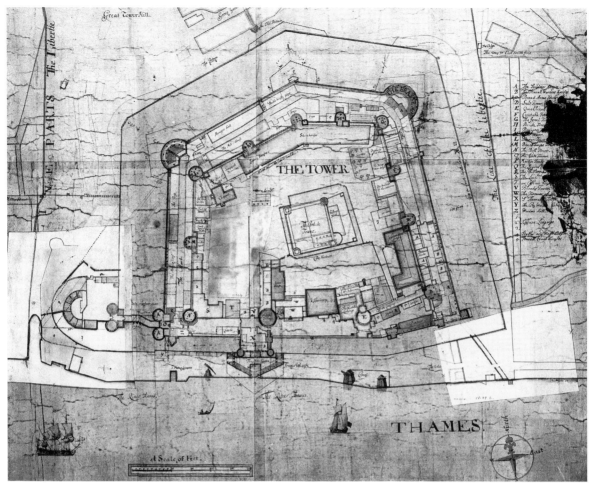

58 *Plan of the Tower in 1682. This survey accompanied a report on the condition of the Tower presented to Charles II in February 1682. It provides the earliest topographical view of property division within the walls and can be regarded as the oldest accurate two-dimensional plan of the castle. Rather mysteriously the drawing shows a large triangular bastion on the Wharf in front of St Thomas's Tower. No such structure ever stood here and no further documentary reference to it is known (Royal Armouries).*

occasional repair. The size of the garrison seems to have declined during this time and with it the demand for accommodation. In 1696 most of the lodgings within Legge's Mount and one of the barrack blocks in the Irish Mint, evidently that erected during the 1680s, were handed over to the Mint for use in the recoinage operation then underway. In 1700, for purely aesthetic reasons, the main guard building, erected only fourteen years earlier, was demolished after the Lords Justices decided that it impaired the 'Beauty and Prospect' of the Grand Storehouse.

Buildings maintained by the Office of Works

Compared to the energetic building record of the Ordnance during the later Stuart period, that of the Office of Works appears trivial. In the years immediately after the Restoration the Office resumed maintenance of some of the old palace buildings against the south side of the White Tower, though the practice was abandoned in 1668 as the redevelopment of the area by the Ordnance began in earnest. Thereafter the Office concentrated its efforts on the lodgings of the Constable, Lieutenant and lesser officers of the Tower, as well as lodgings assigned to Yeoman Warders and prisoners,

79

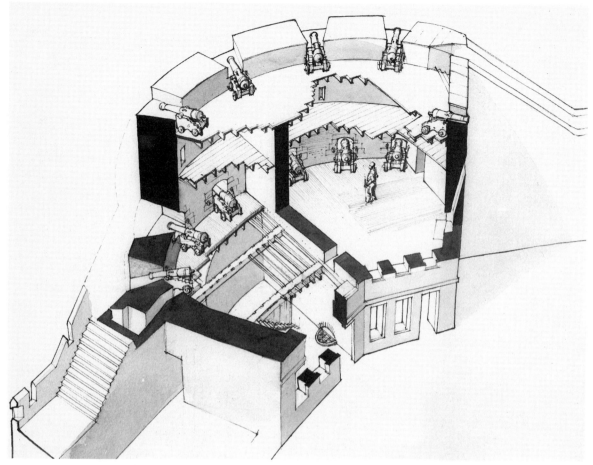

59 *Cut-away illustration of Legge's Mount as it might have appeared in 1683 after being enlarged to accommodate two tiers of guns (Terry Ball).*

together with the Chapel of St Peter ad Vincula, the Menagerie, Record Office and Jewel Office.

Expenditure on these buildings rarely exceeded £1000 per annum and only a few of the more notable operations need be mentioned here. These included the enlargement of the Lieutenant's Lodgings in 1663–4, with the building of two timber-framed rooms. One, 6.4 by 6m (21 ft by 19 ft) was for the Lieutenant, the other 4.5 by 2.75m (15 ft by 9 ft), was for his secretary. These can be identified as the two ground-floor rooms that occupy the angle of the Queen's House, though alterations carried out during the eighteenth and nineteenth centuries have left little evidence of their original appearance. In 1670–1, the walls of the Chapel of St

60 *Engraving of the Chapel of St Peter ad Vincula published in 1737. The house of the chaplain can be seen to the left and the south-west corner of the Grand Storehouse to the right (English Heritage).*

Peter ad Vincula were repaired and the diminutive west tower rebuilt (**60**). Subsequently, in 1675–6, the interior was refitted with, amongst other things, a new pulpit, reading-desk and reredos (**61**). The joinery was performed by Thomas Kinward, and Henry Phillips provided the decorative carvings. Sadly all their work fell victim to the restorations of 1876–7 (see below, p. 104).

61 *Interior of the Chapel of St Peter ad Vincula during the first half of the nineteenth century showing the baroque altar screen and box pews* (Guildhall Library).

11

The Hanoverians

After the prolific building activity of the later seventeenth century the early years of the eighteenth century were relatively quiet. The reappointment of the Duke of Marlborough as Master General of the Ordnance in October 1714 and the Jacobite insurrection that broke out the following year, however, signalled the start of renewed works at the Tower, part of a bustle of military activity that can be detected throughout the country.

Ordnance stores and lodgings
Between 1715 and 1717 considerable efforts were made to improve the storage facilities in and about the White Tower. In February 1715 the Board ordered the western basement to be fitted out to receive saltpetre purchased from the East India Company and two months later the floor of the eastern compartment was ordered to be lowered to provide additional space (**colour plate 9**). The storage of large quantities of this volatile material explains the subsequent introduction, in 1730, of the existing brick vaults in the east and west rooms.

On 8 March 1715, in a move that was to have a significant impact on the appearance of the White Tower, the Surveyor General, Brigadier Michael Richards, was instructed to provide whatever new windows he considered necessary to render the building more useful for the lodging of stores. As a consequence the medieval openings to the ground and uppermost floors were considerably enlarged and fitted with the existing Portland stone (see **7**), Romanesque-style, architraves which many writers have erroneously attributed to Sir Christopher Wren (the windows on the first floor were formed to the same pattern later in the eighteenth century). Those lighting the

eastern ground-floor room still contain their original wooden frames with contemporary hinges and fittings. Four new doorways, with matching stone surrounds, were also formed in the north front at this time to allow easier movement of stores in and out of the building (**62**); the two at ground-floor level still retain their original oak-panelled doors and iron hinges.

As work on the White Tower got underway, so did a general repair and refurbishment of the former medieval wardrobe annexed to its east front. By the early eighteenth century the building had become a store for gunpowder and swords, but now the ground floor was to be converted into a Small Gun Office and Modelling Room with the upper floor fitted out as a Record Office and Drawing Room. By the beginning of 1716 work was sufficiently well advanced to allow the transfer of small arms into the building from the reception sheds that had been erected about the White Tower and down the east side of Coldharbour in 1685–6. Deemed defective and beyond repair these structures, together with the palisade installed around the White Tower during the reign of Charles II, were then demolished and in their place new Ordnance buildings were erected in 1717. These included a new main guard house against the west face of the White Tower, a storehouse for gun carriages against the south front, and down the east side of Coldharbour an extension to the Ordnance administrative office. All three buildings, but particularly the guard house (**63**), displayed something of the plain, bold, almost medieval style of architecture that pervaded Ordnance building design at this time. For many years now this style of military architecture has been known as

62 *(Above) A drawing of the White Tower in 1782 from the north-east, showing the great stone annex attributed to Edward III (British Library).*

63 *(Below) Ground plan and elevation of the Main Guard erected against the west face of the White Tower in 1717 (British Library).*

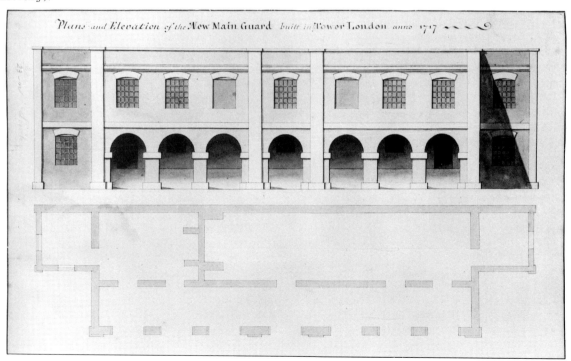

Plans and Elevation of the New Main Guard built in Tower London anno 1717

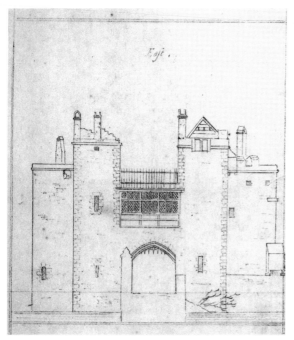

64 *Rear of the Middle Tower showing the timber-framing that was removed during the restorations of 1717–19. Drawing by Clement Lemprière, 1717* (Public Record Office).

'Ordnance Vanbrugh' on account of obvious visual similarities with the work of Sir John Vanbrugh, though recent research indicates that the style probably derived from a design by Nicholas Hawksmoor for the Ordnance barrack block at Berwick-upon-Tweed.

In 1715 the dilapidated state of the Middle Tower, by now the official residence of the Ordnance Barrack Master, gave rise to concern and in an effort to render the building more secure some of the defective battlements were taken down. More radical measures were to follow, however, and between 1717 and 1719 extensive restorations were carried out which gave the building the appearance it retains to this day. Work saw the removal of the medieval framing to the rear of the gate-tower (**64**), the partial refacing of the exterior walls with Portland stone and the introduction of round-headed windows, similar to those installed in the White Tower. The arms of George I over the gate-passage date from this period, being carved by Thomas Green for the sum of £36 (**colour plate 10**). Elsewhere in the Tower several completely new domestic lodgings for

Ordnance officials were built. The most imposing, and now the only survivor, being the so-called Old Hospital Block located immediately north of the New Armouries Building (see **43**). This elegant brick range, intended to house four clerks, was built in 1718–19 at an estimated cost of nearly £3000.

The fortifications and the garrison in the eighteenth century

Immediately after his reappointment as Master General of the Ordnance, in 1714, the Duke of Marlborough ordered the replacement of many of the by-now decayed timber gun platforms that had been installed on the walls of the inner and outer defences in 1682–3. As work began, the Surveyor General, Michael Richards, produced a report in which the effectiveness of the batteries was reconsidered and the greater part of them judged to be of 'no more than appearance'. All the guns along the inner line were deemed 'intirely useless', their weight being too great for the walls. Moreover, it was thought also that the stability of numerous buildings attached to the walls would be endangered if the guns were actually fired. Along the riverside, the battery on St Thomas's Tower was found to be of little use since the building was not vaulted, while the 'Devils' (Develin) Tower on the south-east corner, was considered incapable of accommodating guns and would have to be rebuilt if used for that purpose. Faced with an estimate of £6442 for replacing seemingly impotent defences, together with the substantial cost of their annual maintenance, the order to replace the platforms was quickly rescinded. In future all the batteries were to be concentrated on the outer defences. Even here the total number of guns was to be reduced from 118 to 45, a figure, it was observed, that 'most Strong Towns in Europe have constantly mounted either in Peace or war'.

In April 1752 the accommodation of the Tower garrison came to the fore again after the Irish Barracks, the principal lodgings in the Outer Ward between the Salt and Broad Arrow towers, was found to be in an extremely poor structural state, the whole building being sustained only by a series of inserted posts. The timber building, erected in 1669–70, was deemed beyond repair and a new barrack block was therefore ordered to be constructed on the site. The new building, designed by the Ordnance engineer Dugal Campbell, was a plain,

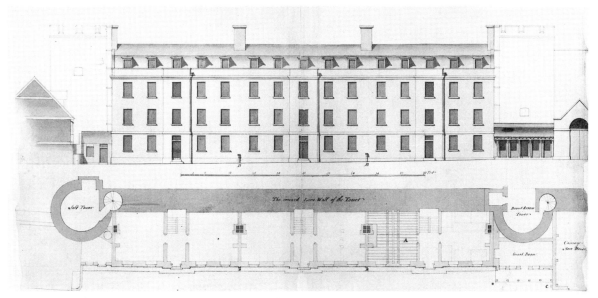

65 *Plan and elevation of the Irish Barracks by Dugal Campbell, 1755* (Public Record Office).

but well proportioned block measuring some 48 by 7m (157 by 22 ft) and comprising three storeys and attic (**65**). Campbell also appears to have been responsible for the design and construction of further soldiers' accommodation at the western entrance, in the form of the Spur Barracks erected on ground made available by infilling part of the moat around the Lion Tower. At the same time a new guard house, the Spur Guard, was erected just north of the Middle Tower (**colour plate 10**).

The waterworks

In 1715 the Tower's water supply was again examined by the Ordnance and in that year the Board ordered a new engine to be installed in the mill at Traitors' Gate. Made by a certain John Rowley 'Master of Mechanicks' for £348 15s 7d, its installation was accompanied by the introduction of a great new lead cistern on the roof of the White Tower which, according to a survey of 1754, held no less than 8215 gallons (31,100 litres) of water. A contract let by the Ordnance in 1755 records that the reservoir could be supplied with sufficient water by working the engine with three to four horses, about three hours a day, four times every fortnight. In 1724 the mill at Traitors' Gate was taken down and rebuilt. When reinstated, the engine was fitted with additional

gears to enable it to drive machinery set up in a room constructed beneath the first floor of St Thomas's Tower for 'Boring Small Gun Barrels' (**66**). A survey prepared by Clement Lemprière in January 1735 shows the arrangement (**67**). The survey appears to have been linked to the introduction of the Tower Infirmary into the western half of the building, thereby replacing the barrack accommodation established here in 1683. The site of the Tower Infirmary immediately prior to 1735 is not clear, but during the 1680s it is known to have been located in a house in Broad Street outside the Tower.

No further alterations of any significance appear to have been carried out in and about St Thomas's Tower until 1806 when the horse-mill was replaced by a steam engine. An apartment at the eastern end of the building, which had been occupied by a Yeoman Warder from at least the time of the Civil War, had to be vacated so that part of the structure could be cut away to receive the new machine. It is interesting to note that the steam-engine keeper was expected to live 'close to the Engine under the same Roof' in the same way that the keeper of the horse-mill had done before him. It was evidently at this time that the rear of the basin was infilled, the old medieval defensive walls demolished and the existing retaining wall and steps introduced.

The Office of Works

As with the later Stuart period the building record of the Office of Works up until the first

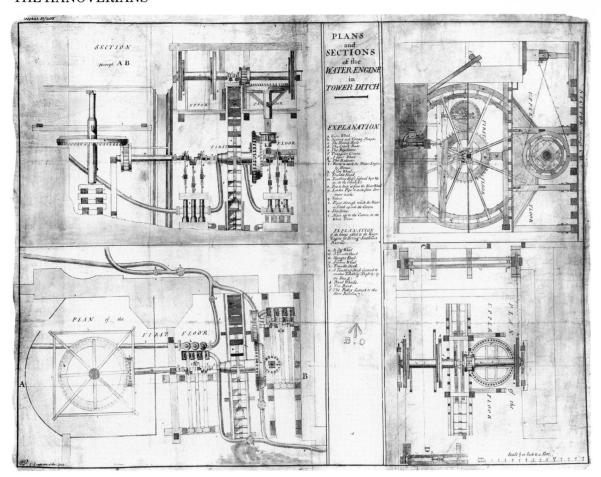

66 *Plans and sections of the Water Engine below St Thomas's Tower by Clement Lemprière, 1725* (Public Record Office).

half of the nineteenth century was not extensive. The condition of the Jewel House in the north-east corner of the Inner Ward was a source of concern during the early eighteenth century and certain outbuildings were demolished on the basis that they stood too close to the Grand Storehouse. As a consequence a new kitchen and wash-house were built for the Jewel Keeper, James Brunwell, in 1721. Three years later, after prolonged negotiations, the Ordnance and the Office of Works agreed to share the cost of providing new stairs to Brunwell's apartment on the first floor of the Martin Tower. The existing structure, the lower part remodelled in 1840, dates from this time.

More considerable works appear to have been carried out in the areas appropriated to the Record Office. John Strype, in his revised addition of Stow's *Survey of London* published in 1720, refers to works carried out in the upper chamber of the Wakefield Tower and part of the adjoining old medieval chamber block to the east, where the main entrance to the depository was located. He notes that some £2000 was spent on repairs and improvements which included the introduction of enlarged sashed windows to let in more light and fine wainscotting 'which is framed into presses round the rooms wherein which are shelves & repositories for the reception of records'. A date of 1728 cut into an ashlar on the south-west face of

67 *Plans and section of St Thomas's Tower by Clement Lemprière, 1735* (Public Record Office).

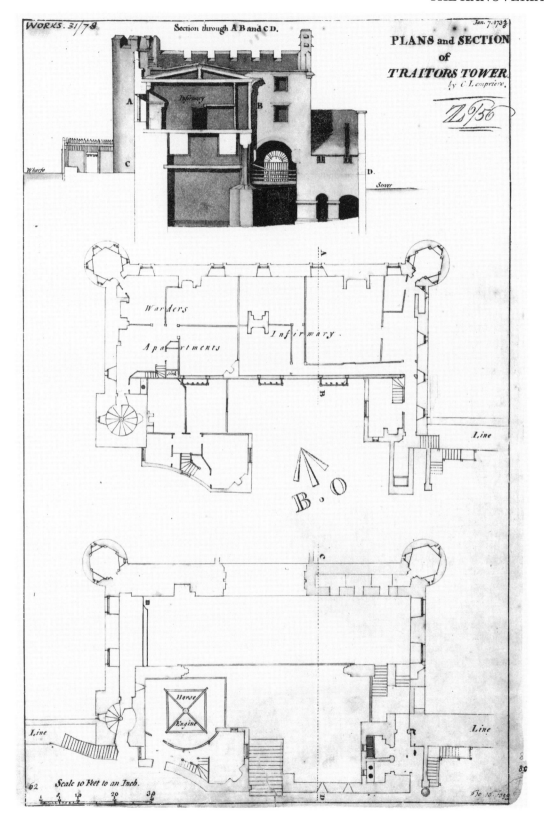

WORKS. 31/78

Section through A B and C D.

Jan. 7. 1733

PLANS and SECTION
of
TRAITORS TOWER.
by C. Lempriere.

Z 56

Infirmary

A

B

Wharfe

C

D

River

Warders

Apartments

Infirmary

Line

B. O

Line

Horse Engine

Line

62   Scale 10 Feet to an Inch.

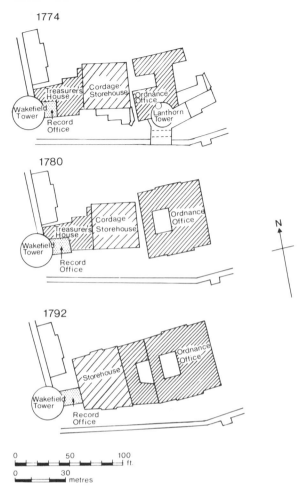

68 *The development of the south side of the Inmost Ward, 1774–92* (English Heritage).

the Wakefield Tower suggests that a partial refacing of the building followed some years later.

In 1736, after more than twenty years of intermittent negotiations with the Ordnance, the Record Office finally secured a large room in the White Tower to accommodate the ever-increasing number of Chancery documents that were being sent to the Tower. The room was on the uppermost floor, adjoining the north side of the Chapel, which had long been used for storing records. The Office of Works fitted out the chamber with wooden presses and shelves at a cost of £314.

In 1749 the Office of Works pulled down the Chaplain's lodgings near the west end of the Chapel of St Peter ad Vincula and on the same site built a three-storeyed house which survives to this day (see **55**). Six years earlier they had

collaborated with the Office of Ordnance in the partial reconstruction of the thirteenth-century chamber block adjoining the west side of the Lanthorn Tower. The top floor formed part of the Major of the Garrison's apartments, centered on the Lanthorn Tower, while the two floors below were occupied by the Ordnance and were integrated with their administrative office to the north. This awkward division of responsibility was resolved in 1776 after fire had badly damaged the Lanthorn Tower and some adjoining buildings. The Major's lodgings were surrendered to the Ordnance, who in return handed over the house hitherto assigned to their Treasurer to the west of the old medieval great hall (**68**). The exchange was to some extent made easy by the fact that the Major had already left the lodgings to take up residence in the Queen's House (where his official descendants reside to this day).

The rebuilding of the Ordnance Office

Some idea of the scale of the fire that gutted the Lanthorn Tower and its environs on 2 January 1774 is provided by the number of men who attended the blaze from outside the fortress. Altogether the various fire offices and parishes sent 267 men; engines came from the Navy Office and the parishes of St Katherine's, All Hallows, Barking and St Dunstan. The fire not only resulted in an exchange of property, but also led to the single largest building operation seen at the Tower during the eighteenth century – the construction of a new Ordnance Office in Coldharbour. The old building had not in fact been seriously damaged during the fire, but the Board of Ordnance clearly seized on the occasion as an opportunity to provide themselves with new prestigious quarters.

The demolitions that preceded construction of the new office saw the removal of much of what remained of the old medieval and Tudor palace. This included the vestiges of the sixteenth-century Queen's Lodgings embedded in the heart of the Ordnance Office; the thirteenth-century Lanthorn Tower and its adjoining chamber block; most of Edward III's gatehouse midway between the Lanthorn and Salt towers, together with the section of curtain wall to the west, as well as that part of Henry VII's gallery which rested on it. Demolished also was a gatehouse spanning the Outer Ward to the south of the Lanthorn Tower, whose origins appear to date back to the

69 *The arms of the Board of Ordnance that were positioned over the main entrance of the Ordnance office in 1779. Now mounted on the south wall of the New Armouries Building* (photo: Jeremy Hall, Royal Armouries).

time of Edward III, together with a slender tower to the south known as the Brick Tower. Finally, the upper floor of the Cradle Tower was removed, possibly for no other reason than it was thought to obstruct the view of the new building from the river. The order to commence demolitions was issued in December 1776. The dangerous condition of the Lanthorn Tower, however, had resulted in it being 'pulled down so low as to make it entirely safe' six months earlier.

As operations got underway, the most immediate problem to arise was the disposal of large amounts of building debris that began to accumulate on the site. A scheme to remove the rubbish by water was abandoned after being deemed slow and expensive. Consequently it was decided to cart the material out of the Tower and deposit it within the Liberties. The plan was delayed by the Resident Governor who objected to the builders using the newly constructed East Drawbridge which, together with its gateway, had been built in 1774 at an estimated cost of £495. In the event, however, some 11,000 cart-loads of rubbish were conveyed over the bridge and spread over Little Tower Hill on the east side of the fortress.

The new office, which was evidently ready for occupation in the autumn of 1780, was a handsome building designed in the prevailing neo-classical style of the day. It measured 32 by 33m (105 by 100 ft) and comprised two storeys and a rusticated basement around a small courtyard. The main entrance was located in the north front behind a portico surmounted by the martial arms of the Board of Ordnance (**69**).

On 23 July 1788, only eight years after completion, the new office was seriously damaged by fire. As with the conflagration of 1774, the scale of the blaze is illustrated by the fact that no less than 257 men and 13 appliances were dispatched from various offices and parishes to help the Ordnance's own fire-fighting team, who, together with soldiers from the garrison and a team of workmen, tried to combat the blaze. The 'reforming and rebuilding' of the office was underway by January 1789; work was to take four years to complete. The operation involved not only a complete recasting of the interior, but the extension of the building by 14m (45 ft) to the west at the expense of Henry III's great hall, which formed the carcass of the Cordage Storehouse. A new storehouse was erected to the west of the enlarged office on ground made available by pulling down the old Ordnance Treasury House (see **68**). This had been transferred to the Lieutenant of the Tower in 1776, but there is no evidence that he actually lived there and in 1783 he offered the building back to the Ordnance in order that it could be used to accommodate officers of the Royal Regiment of Artillery.

Also dating from the late eighteenth century is a range of brick buildings erected by the Mint

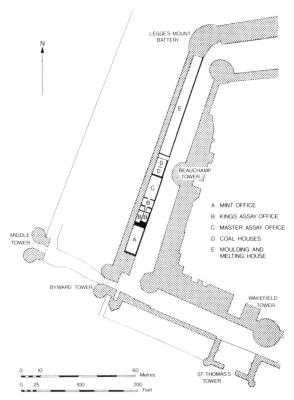

N

LEGGE'S MOUNT
BATTERY

BEAUCHAMP
TOWER

E

D
D
C
B
B
B/B
A

A MINT OFFICE
B KINGS ASSAY OFFICE
C MASTER ASSAY OFFICE
D COAL HOUSES
E MOULDING AND
   MELTING HOUSE

MIDDLE
TOWER

BYWARD TOWER

WAKEFIELD
TOWER

ST THOMAS'S
TOWER

0   10   60
              Metres
0   25   100   200
              Feet

70 *Plan showing the surviving late eighteenth-century Mint buildings in the western Outer Ward* (English Heritage).

against the outer curtain wall between Legge's Mount and the Byward Tower (**70**). These appear to be the last buildings constructed by the department before coin production was transferred to a more commodious site on Little Tower Hill in 1812. Although much altered in the nineteenth and twentieth centuries these buildings now stand as the only substantive evidence for the Mint at the Tower.

The fortifications and the garrison in the nineteenth century

The departure of the Mint led to something of a scramble in the Outer Ward, with the Army, Ordnance Office, Record Office and the Constable all laying claims to the vacated buildings. Although it was probably not content with the final distribution, the Army acquired several of the larger buildings, which were then converted into lodgings for the garrison. The size of the garrison had been increasing since the late eighteenth century. Pressure for

additional accommodation became particularly intense during the Napoleonic Wars and in 1804 the Irish Barracks was extended 27m (88 ft) northwards, into an area traditionally controlled by the Mint, in an effort to meet demand.

Despite repairs and adjustments the old Mint buildings provided unsatisfactory accommodation for the garrison. The problem was finally resolved with the construction of a great new barrack block on the site of the Grand Storehouse which was consumed by fire during the early hours of 31 October 1841. It was the Duke of Wellington who, as constable of the Tower for 26 years until his death in 1852, was largely responsible for seeing the barracks built. Work began on the foundations during the early months of 1845 and on 14 June, amidst much ceremony, the Duke laid the foundation stone of the building – the name of which was to celebrate his greatest victory – the Waterloo Barracks (**71**). The barracks was originally intended to house 826 men, but this was increased to nearly 1000. The architectural style was described as 'castellated Gothic of the fifteenth century'. The author of the design is not readily apparent, though all the drawings (including rejected versions) were prepared by the Ordnance Royal Engineers, and it is possible that their Commander, Major Hall, played a leading role.

In addition to the Waterloo Barracks the Royal Engineers provided separate officers' quarters, now the museum of the Royal Fusiliers, to the north-east of the White Tower. The site had been occupied by a pair of fine brick houses erected for the Surveyor and Clerk of the Ordnance in 1699–1701, and the initial scheme envisaged a refurbishment of the building with gothic windows and other enrichments being applied to the existing elevations. Subsequent designs, however, indicate a new building. There is some doubt as to extent to which the radical solution was pursued, since the plan of the extant building follows very closely that of the Stuart structure, while early brickwork can be identified in the base of the south wall.

When work on the Waterloo Barracks and Officers' Block was finished, the role of the Duke of Wellington was acknowledged by the erection of a statue of the Duke on the parade ground before the two buildings (see **71**). The gesture was not altogether successful. The statue was described as 'poor and pompous' and

71 *Mid-nineteenth-century engraving of the Waterloo Barracks with the statue of the Duke of Wellington in the foreground* (Royal Armouries).

in 1863 was moved down to the Royal Arsenal at Woolwich where it resides to this day.

The Duke of Wellington's preoccupation with security also resulted in the last major attempt to modernize the Tower's defences. Surprisingly little had been attempted since the gun batteries were reduced in the early eighteenth century. The moat continued to create maintenance problems, which the construction of a brick counterscarp wall around the outer edge (on the line of the existing railings) in 1789–90 did little to relieve. Sir George Cathcart, who as Lieutenant Governor carried out an investigation into the state of the Tower and its defences for the Duke of Wellington, came to the conclusion that it was in fact the mud and stagnant water of the moat that was to a large extent responsible for the poor health of the Tower garrison. As a consequence the moat was drained in 1843; it was levelled to provide a parade ground and even on occasion a sheep pasture. It was also at this time that a direct supply route was re-established from the Wharf to the White Tower crossing the moat at the same point as the short-lived bridge of

1667. The new bridge, the Middle Drawbridge, has since been replaced by an early twentieth-century structure. Munitions and other stores were conveyed along a tramway that passed through the late eighteenth-century storehouse to the east of the Wakefield Tower and along an underground tunnel before entering the basement of the White Tower near the south-west corner.

In response to a report prepared by the Engineer Department in 1845 and a very real fear on the part of the authorities that a Chartist mob would attempt to storm the Tower, the west and north outer curtain walls were extensively repaired between 1848 and 1852. Most of the existing loop-holes, gun emplacements and musketry arrangements along the lines were created at this time. On the exposed salient midway between Legge's Mount and Brass Mount a projecting timber sentinel box was replaced by a massive stone tower known as the North Bastion (see **90**). At the Brass Mount a spiral staircase and passage were built in the core of the earth infill to provide access into the ground-floor gallery from the roof platform. This seems to have replaced a simple flight of steps that was introduced about 1715. A reduction in political tension and lack of funds meant that work on the more dilapidated east wall did not start until 1862. Here the curtain is crowned with a high

72 *Photograph taken during the 1860s looking towards the rear of the Bloody Tower with the Main Guard and its entrance colonnade to the left* (English Heritage).

arcaded parapet, intended to protect troops from any musketry fire from the lofty warehouses of St Katherine's Docks to the east.

Within the walls very considerable works, other than those associated with the Waterloo Barracks and Officers' Block, were begun in 1846. These were the product of a desire for modernization and improvement that seems to have gripped the Ordnance in the years leading up to its abolition in 1855, but inevitably the guiding hand of the Duke of Wellington was never far away. A new Main Guard was created out of the storehouse erected in 1670–1 to the north of the Wakefield Tower. The old structure was gutted, an extra storey added and a new entrance punched through the medieval curtain wall which formed its west elevation (**72**). The latter was embellished with

what H. W. Brewer described as a 'kind of open arcade of the most dismal design' erected at the expense of the picturesque row of timber-framed buildings dating from the time of Henry VIII (see **37**). When the new guard was occupied, the old one, erected in 1717 against the west face of the White Tower, was demolished and the ground level raised and terraced.

The year 1846 also saw the demolition of certain privately-owned public houses whose services were replaced by military canteens. Two of the best known inns were the Stone Kitchen (**73**) and the Golden Chain (**74**). The former occupied a range of buildings over the thirteenth-century cross wall and gate immediately west of the Bell Tower (it might be mentioned that the cross wall and its gate on the south side of the Bell Tower, supporting an inn called the Bunch of Grapes, was demolished in 1796). The latter stood to the west of the Salt Tower and its demolition was accompanied by that of the remaining section of Henry III's south curtain wall and that part of Henry VII's

The Celebrated Canteen, in the Tower of London
Called The "Stone Kitchen"

Now being demolished
Sep 1846

See Morning advertiser
Sep. 11th

73 *The Stone Kitchen tavern which stood immediately west of the Bell Tower. A drawing by T. H. Shepherd shortly before demolition of the building in 1846* (Guildhall Library).

74 *The Golden Chain tavern which stood against the south side of Henry III's curtain wall immediately west of the Salt Tower. A drawing by T.H. Shepherd shortly before demolition of the building in 1846 (see also* **78***) (Guildhall Library).*

gallery which rested on it (see **78**). In addition the northern half of another late thirteenth-century cross wall and gate between the Salt Tower and Well Tower was pulled down together with various old buildings around it. These operations formed part of the programme recommended by the Engineer Department in 1845 to clear the Outer Ward and during the next few years most of the old buildings against the face of the inner circuit were pulled down and the curtain wall restored. Delays were experienced with the west wall, however, since the Jewel House immediately to the south of the Martin Tower could not be demolished until 1870, while the lack of storage space meant that the Irish Barracks to the south was left standing until 1878.

Further demolitions were to follow at the western entrance. The last of the wild animals in the Royal Menagerie had been moved to Regents Park in 1835 after a lion was accused of biting a soldier. The Keeper, Mr Kops, was entitled to stay in his house for life, so that it was not until his death in 1853 that demolition of his house, the Lion Tower and the various other old menagerie buildings could proceed (**colour plate 11**). The clearance also included the mid eighteenth-century Spur Barracks and Spur Guard, and a building attached to the south side of the Middle Tower assigned to the Gentleman Porter (**colour plate 10**), the last in a line of such lodgings in this area dating back to the fifteenth century. On the cleared site, almost opposite the Middle Tower, a Ticket Office was constructed to a design prepared by the Royal Engineers. This was a single-storeyed structure with a cast-iron frame.

The Small Gun Office
During the 1860s the eastern half of the Wharf was cleared of a tangle of Ordnance workshops and stores. Their removal saw the last provision for the proving and manufacturing of small arms disappear from the Tower. The origins of the proof yard on the Wharf date

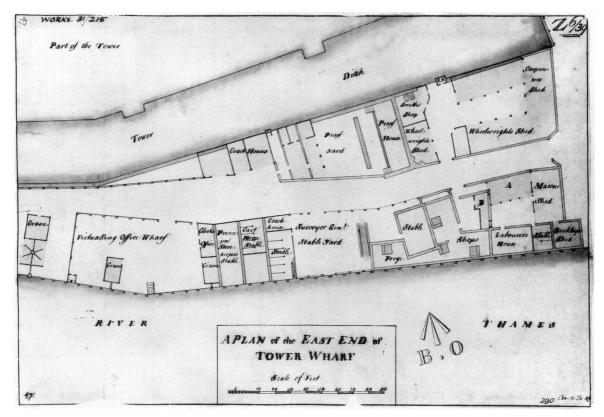

75 *Plan of the eastern part of the Wharf in 1742* (Public Record Office).

back to 1682 when the Ordnance built a 'Proofe house and Chargeing house' there, to replace their earlier facilities lost with the sale of the Artillery Ground in the Minories to the north of the Tower (**75**). The Small Gun Office at this time did not supervise a 'manufactory', rather the furbishers and gunsmiths were on the whole concerned with the checking and finishing of parts supplied by outside contractors. After the old Ordnance administrative office behind the Chapel of St Peter's was vacated in 1673, the Furbisher of Small Arms seems to have established himself on the site. In April 1715 an estimate was prepared for 'rebuilding Shops for the Furbishers & Gunsmiths to work in at or about Deverells [Devereux] Tower'. Further facilities were set up in the Flint and Bowyer towers in 1718; one tower being fitted out for 'stocking' the other for 'Lock hardening'. In addition there were forges in the Mint and on the Wharf, while the barrel-boring bench at St Thomas's Tower has already been mentioned.

The outbreak of the Napoleonic Wars and the enormous increase in the demand for guns was more than the existing Ordnance supply system could cope with, so an 'Arms Manufactory' employing hundreds of people was established at the eastern end of the Wharf around the old Proof House. The factory closed in 1815 when the Office's manufacturing facilities were transferred to Enfield and Lewisham. The buildings, however, were left standing to house the department's workshops, much to the annoyance of the military engineers who throughout the first half of the nineteenth century repeatedly called for their demolition in order to improve the defences of the Tower.

The Small Gun Office seems to have continued its activities behind the Chapel of St Peter's and along the inner north curtain until the disastrous fire of 1841. The fire, in fact, began in one of their workshops within the upper floor of the Bowyer Tower from where it spread to the roof of the Grand Storehouse. Apart from these two buildings the blaze badly damaged the Brick and Flint towers, the latter having only been rebuilt by the Ordnance 45 years earlier. Both towers, together with the

76 *The Horse Armoury against the south side of the White Tower during the course of demolition in 1883* (English Heritage).

upper chamber of the Bowyer Tower were rebuilt a few years later, but they were to be occupied by the garrison, rather than the Small Gun Office, whose operations during its final years at the Tower were restricted to the buildings at the end of the Wharf.

The Horse Armoury and New Jewel House
In an age when tourist interest in the Tower was steadily increasing, two buildings erected by the Ordnance during the first half of the nineteenth century deserve particular mention. The first was the Horse Armoury, built in 1825 against the south face of the White Tower on a site previously occupied by the 1717 Carriage Storehouse (**76**). The Horse Armoury was specially constructed to house the Line of Kings, which the great armour expert, Dr Samuel Meyrick, sought to rearrange in a more

scientific manner. However, he expressed annoyance at not having been consulted about the building's design, which appears to have been the work of the then Ordnance Clerk of Works at the Tower, a certain Mr Wright. The building was a low, crenellated, single-storeyed structure some 46 m (150 ft) long and 10 m (33 ft) wide, excluding the three towers which projected from its south elevation. Four circular windows were glazed with decorative glass, two featuring armorial devices, while the lavish interior was aisled with imitation Norman columns, evidently copies of those found in the chapel within the White Tower. Clearly the building was intended to harmonize with the architecture of the White Tower and its annex to the east, though Thomas Allen in his *History and Antiquities of London* published in 1827 regretted 'that the Government should have allowed a paltry building like that of the New Horse Armoury to have been erected against the venerable and noble White Tower' while a commentator writing in the *Builder* in July

77 *The new Jewel House in 1841* (Royal Armouries).

1851 thought the 'perpetrator' of the design 'deserved to be beheaded'.

The second building erected by the Ordnance, again in a gothic style, was the New Jewel House. Responsibility for the Regalia was vested in the Lord Chamberlain's Office, but, under an unusual arrangement with the Ordnance, the Royal Engineers designed and constructed the Jewel House with their costs to be reimbursed with surplus fees from public admission charges. The building adjoined the south side of the Martin Tower (the old Jewel Office) with its elaborate crenellated entrance and flanking towers within the Inner Ward (**77**), but with the actual strong-room standing on a brick vault within the Outer Ward. The rooms for the Jewel Keeper and his family were over the Jewel Chamber and communicated with the Martin Tower which acted as an extension to the Keeper's quarters. The new building, which opened to the public early in 1842, proved to be anything but a success. It was plagued with defects and the rooms were constantly damp. The lighting of the Jewel Chamber proved inadequate and Argan lamps had to be installed. Inspections revealed that the building was not properly fire-proofed or secure against theft. Less than ten years after it had been opened, and despite remedial measures, the Lord Chamberlain announced that the building was still unsatisfactory and in 1852 the aged Duke of Wellington declared that it would have to be pulled down since no other use could be found for it (though a role as a prison was considered). Demolition meant the relocation of the Regalia to the Wakefield Tower in 1870. The Ordnance, for its part, never received a penny towards the cost of constructing the ill-fated building.

12

The remedievalization of the castle

Against a background of increasing antiquarian interest and a growing appreciation of medieval architecture, the Tower in the second half of the nineteenth century assumed more and more the status of an historic monument. This new role was created at the expense of the various departments of state which had traditionally operated within its walls. The exodus of these offices, as already mentioned, began with the Mint in 1812 and continued with the departure of the Royal Menagerie in 1835. The Record Office withdrew during the 1850s, but it was the gradual phasing out of the manufactory and storage facilities of the War Office (who assumed the duties of the Ordnance Office in 1855) in the wake of the Crimean War, which saw the largest areas of the fortress vacated. As areas were freed the older buildings were repaired as part of an on-going programme of restoration carried out by the Office of Works.

The work of Anthony Salvin

The architect appointed by the Office to oversee much of the restoration was Anthony Salvin, a leading exponent of the Later Gothic Revival and widely admired for his earlier restorations at Newark, Carisbrooke and Caernarvon castles. Salvin was first consulted about the Beauchamp Tower (**colour plate 4**) as the collection of commemorative inscriptions carved on the walls of the first floor by famous prisoners during the sixteenth and seventeenth centuries had led Harrison Ainsworth to suggest that it be opened to the public. Salvin surveyed the building in April 1851, but nothing seems to have happened until the following year when two Warders' houses against the east face were pulled down. Thereafter the exterior walls were refaced, windows and doorways replaced and battlements recreated. The operation was a triumph for Salvin, being widely reported in the press and applauded by the Tower authorities, particularly the Lieutenant-Governor, Lord del Ros, whose *Memorials of the Tower of London* published in 1866 is peppered with admiring comments about the architect and his work.

The next commission Salvin was to receive concerned the Salt Tower. The fabric of the tower had suffered somewhat over the years and when, in 1846, various adjoining buildings were demolished it was found that areas of stonework had been poorly replaced in brick (**78**). The Constable, Lord Combermere, informed Queen Victoria of its condition and on 14 June 1855 Prince Albert paid a visit of inspection. In the Prince Consort's opinion the restoration needed to be part of a comprehensive plan for the Tower, carried out by a single architect. This was to be Salvin and work on the Salt Tower, which was carried out in 1857–8, followed closely the pattern established at the Beauchamp Tower.

Prince Albert's call for greater control over future building works at the Tower resulted in the introduction of a procedure whereby royal approval was required before any works could begin. It was Lord del Ros, who with a major confrontation with the War Office looming, was especially keen to see the rule operating, and it was evidently he who drew the attention of the

78 *The Golden Chain tavern and part of Henry III's curtain wall being demolished in 1846. From a watercolour by J.W. Archer* (English Heritage).

79 *Part of the range of Casemates along the north side of the Outer Ward showing the change from brick* (left) *to stone facings* (photo: Garry Kennard, Royal Armouries).

Prince to past precedent for royal approval. The issue which brought the Tower authorities and the War Office into conflict was the construction of the Casemates against the rear of the outer curtain wall. Work on these bomb-vaulted structures had started in 1853, but the Crimean War necessitated the temporary retention of the old Mint buildings for storage purposes, thus only the Casemates between Legge's Mount and the North Bastion were erected before work was suspended. In 1856 the War Office prepared to continue the range as far east as the Brass Mount. However, Lord del Ros intervened, describing the Casemates that had already been constructed as having a 'modern facade of Brickwork . . . which might be handsome for a new Brewery or Factory' but hardly suitable for a medieval castle. He argued, therefore, that not only should the next Casemates be provided with more appropriate elevations, but that those already constructed should be refronted.

The War Office protested that since the building contract had been let before the introduction of the Prince Consort's rule and the general principles adopted by Salvin, the work should be allowed to proceed as planned. In the event a compromise was reached whereby the new Casemates had their elevations built in stone to a style recommended by Salvin, while those already constructed were allowed to stand as they were (**79**). In his *Memorial* Lord del Ros defines the style that Salvin devised for buildings located within the walls as having no defensive character but 'that their fronts and roofs should resemble the common street architecture in London before the Great Fire'. The tussle over the Casemates marked a watershed in the building history of the Tower, from now on historic as well as any aesthetic considerations would transcend all others in determining the appearance of all new buildings or alterations to existing ones.

By April 1858 Sir James Pennethorpe's new Public Record Office in Chancery Lane was sufficiently well advanced to receive the mass of manuscripts and other records held at the Tower. Since 1811 the Record Office had controlled the whole of the uppermost floor in the

White Tower in addition to the Chapel and eastern room on the first floor. The removal of the records came not a minute too soon, for, despite warnings, the War Office continued to store explosives and ammunition in the basements below. Salvin was consulted about the uppermost western room, the so-called Council Chamber in 1856, when it was proposed that it should be fitted out as a small arms store. Work, however, does not seem to have started until 1861. The roof, though the timbers were sound, was considered weak and was supported by a series of posts which would have to be removed since they stood in the way of the proposed arms stands (**colour plate 9**). Salvin removed these and strengthened the roof beams with iron girders and large decorative knellers against the external walls (since removed). The floor was reinforced and a number of new windows provided in the north and west walls. The Chapel was not taken in hand until 1864, when the walls were scoured of all accretions and repaired; the existing windows, featuring shafts and cushion capitals, were installed at this time.

In June 1862 part of the stonework of the south-east turret of St Thomas's Tower collapsed as a result of vibrations emanating from the hydraulic engine. The building was in a dilapidated condition with countless alterations over the centuries having taken a heavy toll. One of the last, and arguably most unusual, adaptations was the boarding up of the rear of the basin by the military authorities in order to provide privacy for the soldiers of the garrison who, for a short time, used the basin as a sort of large bathing pool! Salvin inspected the building and concluded that further structural damage would ensue unless the machinery was relocated. Consequently the tower was shored up and the machinery moved to a new Engine House designed by Salvin and erected at the main western entrance (the present Tower shop). Between 1864 and 1866 St Thomas's Tower was extensively restored to provide the building with the appearance which it retains to this day. Much of the exterior was refaced, the battlements and turrets were reset and new, medieval-style, windows introduced. The Tudor framing to the rear of the building was stripped and the spaces between the timbers infilled with brick noggings, while three large oriel windows were recreated in their original sixteenth-century positions. The positions had

been identified during the course of works.

By September 1866 it had been decided to move the Regalia to the Wakefield Tower which, since the departure of the Record Office a few years earlier, had functioned as a Warder's lodging. Salvin had previously produced designs for a new Jewel House on the site of the 1840–1 building next to the Martin Tower, but in the event it was decided to demolish the troublesome structure and reconstruct the curtain wall instead. The Martin Tower, it should be noted, escaped restoration and to this day retains its eighteenth-century sash windows, with its walls revealing a mixture of brick and stone repairs of various dates – a valuable record of how most of the wall towers must have appeared before Salvin was called in (**80**).

Work on the Wakefield Tower began in 1867. The operation involved the replacement of the original timber first floor with a reinforced brick vault to support the jewel display, the introduction of the existing ceiling vault to the first-floor chamber, the construction of a covered entrance (now demolished) against the north side of the tower, and the provision of the still surviving stone bridge to link the Jewel Chamber with the upper floor of St Thomas's Tower which was converted into a residence for the Jewel Keeper. Messrs Brown & Downing, iron founders of Birmingham provided the great cage, railings, gate and barriers behind which the Regalia were put on display in January 1870 (**81**).

While work on the Wakefield Tower was in progress other projects were in hand elsewhere. Various old buildings to the west of the Bloody Tower were pulled down at the end of 1866 and on part of the site Salvin erected new Warders' houses – the present Nos. 7 and 8 Tower Green. The Bloody Tower was repaired and crenellated and the two windows in the upper floor replaced. Together with the Wakefield Tower these were the last restorations the now elderly Salvin was to direct at the Tower. After twenty years, responsibility for such works was to be entrusted to others. In assessing Salvin's work it might be suggested that the Beauchamp Tower, the earliest of his projects, was perhaps the most successful in terms of attention to detail and quality of work. This might have been linked to the amount of time the architect could spend on any one project; clearly as his reputation grew and demands for his services increased, there must have been an unavoidable

81 *The Crown Jewels as originally displayed in the upper chamber of the Wakefield Tower (Royal Armouries).*

need to delegate more and more. The habit of replacing historic fabric where repair would properly suffice, was an unfortunate, but universal, practice at this time, and not something Salvin can be accused of carrying out to extremes. By the 1880s, however, some of his work was beginning to attract criticism; the scraping away of all the historic plaster from the walls of the Chapel of St John in the White Tower to reveal naked masonry is one action he can justifiably be castigated for, while the loss of the remains of the medieval fresco in the

80 *Martin Tower viewed from the south-east showing a variety of post-medieval repairs and alterations to the original thirteenth-century stonework.* (Photo: Gerry Kennard, Royal Armouries).

oratory at the Wakefield Tower is another. If Salvin was guilty of being heavy-handed on some occasions, on others he showed a willingness to conserve historic fabric, as demonstrated at St Thomas's Tower where he sought additional funds to preserve two doorways found during the course of works, though confessing that they 'can never be made use of again, still I think they should be restored as a piece of history'. For better or worse, Salvin's legacy at the Tower represents an early part of the story of repair and consolidation of historic buildings in this country. These works are among some of the first sponsored by the state and the lessons learnt at the Tower and elsewhere at this time provide the foundations of modern-day technical and archaeological approaches to building conservation.

The work of John Taylor

Although no longer directing operations, this was not the last time Salvin was consulted about works at the Tower. In 1876 he was

103

82 *The interior of the Chapel of St Peter ad Vincula following the restorations of 1876–7. The low stone altar screen was removed in 1970* (Royal Armouries).

asked to comment on some proposals for the Chapel of St Peter ad Vincula and since he was unable to travel up to London from his home in Fenhurst he sent his son instead. Various attempts had been made to renovate the Chapel over the years. In 1841 new pews and benches were installed to increase the seating capacity. Further alterations were carried out in 1862, including the removal of the 'unsightly' Tudor porch against the south front. An old doorway found in the west wall was unblocked and recommissioned, while the plaster ceiling within was removed to expose the Tudor roof timbers. Despite these measures there were more complaints and in March 1864 the Chaplain wrote to the Office of Works protesting that the walls were crumbling with damp and the monuments 'encumbered with filth'.

Three years later Salvin was asked to advise. His proposals were not implemented because of financial restraints imposed on the budget for 1868/9 following the 'extraordinary demands for the Abyssinian Expedition'. Some progress was made after the Royal Engineers produced plans in June 1871 which saw two large undercrofts, originally part of the old Ordnance office lying to the north, converted into amenities for the Chapel. The vault adjacent to the Chapel became the Crypt, that beyond provided storage facilities. Some of Salvin's proposals were incorporated in the principal programme of restoration which was eventually implemented in 1876–7 under the direction of John Taylor, the Office of Works' architect who was now directing restoration works at the Tower. This saw the box pews and an eighteenth-century gallery replaced with benches; the baroque pulpit and reading desk both disappeared, as did the fine contemporary pedimented reredos, which was replaced by a low stone screen (**82**). The present vestry was built to replace a small wooden structure that occupied the south-west corner of the nave, the west tower was heavily restored and some of the exterior walls refaced with a dubious cocktail of knapped flints set in cement (successfully removed from the south front in 1973).

The last visit the elderly Salvin was to make

83 *The White Tower photographed from the south-east shortly before the demolition of the great stone annex in 1879* (Guildhall Library).

to the Tower was in August 1879 at the invitation of John Taylor. Without any reservations Taylor had just demolished the large stone building annexed to the east front of the White Tower whose origins are thought to be associated with the fourteenth-century wardrobe. The building had been given an extra third floor during the early nineteenth century, a move which had further obscured the view of the White Tower and thus attracted antiquarian complaint. Demolition of the southeast corner of the building was halted when it became clear that the masonry contained the remains of the medieval Wardrobe Tower. Taylor seems to have been somewhat surprised by the discovery, though the tower was well known from topographical sources and photographs of the building prior to demolition clearly show the medieval structure standing close to its original height (**83**).

The other area Salvin inspected was the stretch of riverside defences to the east of St Thomas's Tower. Here restoration work included a reconstruction of the missing upper floor of the Cradle Tower, together with the removal of all accretions and unblocking of the river entrance on the floor below. The walls of the upper floor of the Well Tower were largely dismantled, then rebuilt and capped with a concrete roof, while the east and west elevations of the Develin Tower were refaced. The intervening curtain walls were repaired and their seventeenth-century gun ports replaced with imitation medieval crenellations. Lastly, the East Drawbridge was refashioned to its present appearance. Curious designs for a twin-towered gatehouse to be erected on the Wharf in front of the East Drawbridge were also prepared, but the scheme came to nothing.

In 1882 the Office of Works prepared to begin the largest single restoration yet undertaken at the Tower – the 'reconstruction' of the inner defences between the Salt and Wakefield towers. The building then occupying much of the site, the late eighteenth-century Ordnance office, had few admirers and in 1866 the then Lieutenant, Lord del Ros, described it and the adjoining storehouse to the west as having the 'decorative style of the great gin-palaces of London'. Even before its abolition in 1855, the Ordnance had broken with tradition, with the Board ceasing to meet at the Tower, and in 1854, while the Crimean War was raging, an additional third floor was added to the building, which by this time was being used as a storehouse (**84**).

Alarmed by reports of the proposed reconstruction, the Society for the Protection of Ancient Buildings, which was founded by William Morris in 1877 to discourage the sort of over-restoration witnessed along the riverside defences, wrote to the Office of Works in July 1882 to express their opposition to the scheme, arguing that any reproduction would be 'mischievous, illusory and ridiculous'. Moreover, they drew attention to the antiquity of the Record House attached to the east side of the Wakefield Tower (**85**) and argued that under no circumstances should it be demolished to make way for pastiche. The Society judged the construction of the building to be not much later than that of the Wakefield Tower itself. They drew attention to various architectural details including an ornate escutcheon, probably dating to the reign of Charles II, that surmounted the entrance, a stone spiral staircase of medieval construction and fine oak panelling on the first and second floors which had been described by John Strype in 1720. Finally, the

84 *View from the Wharf in 1882 showing, from left to right, the Wakefield Tower, Record Office, late eighteenth-century storehouse and former Ordnance office* (English Heritage).

Society referred to earlier assurances by the Office that no further works were planned at the Tower, but noted that during their site inspection they had seen much new work in progress at the Broad Arrow Tower, while at Legge's Mount the seventeenth-century brickwork was being refaced in stone.

The Society's intervention failed to stop demolition of the former Ordnance office, the vast amount of brick, stone, ironwork and lead fetching the paltry sum of £1320 by way of auction. The need for temporary storage facilities, however, prevented the demolition of the eighteenth-century storehouse and with it the adjoining Record House, at least for the present. To the north, the Horse Armoury was pulled down, during which process a twelfth-century wall that linked the Wardrobe Tower to the south-east corner of the White Tower was found (see **76**). Taylor does seem to have

contemplated its preservation, but in the event demolition proved easier. The only material seemingly retained was some painted glass from the windows of the Horse Armoury, which the Ordnance had obtained from the house of Horace Walpole at Strawberry Hill in 1842. This was placed in the windows of the Chapel of St John in the White Tower where it can still be seen.

Though preparation for the reconstruction of the inner defences proceeded, the Office of Works was at least obliged to justify the reasoning behind the project. An internal memorandum from Taylor to the Works Secretary states that careful examination of the Record House revealed it to be no older than the reign of Charles II, though he did agree that the spiral staircase within was of medieval date. Taylor had removed some plaster from the foot of the stairs and found evidence for the original entrance into the Wakefield Tower, which he decided 'was probably a 15th century insertion in the place of an original arrow slit'. This, and the discovery of old foundations in the basement of the demolished Ordnance office

85 *Photograph of the Wakefield Tower in c.1870 showing the reconstructed bridge to St Thomas's Tower and the entrance to the Record House surmounted by its coat of arms* (English Heritage).

main object and utility of the works no useful purpose would be served by the First Secretary agreeing to an interview with them.

Undeterred the Society obtained permission to visit the Tower again. The visit, as they subsequently informed the Office, only served to convince their Committee that the destruction of the Record House would be a serious mistake. They forwarded structural and documentary evidence which clearly demonstrated the antiquity of the building and set out the nature of the former medieval frontage stretching from the Wakefield Tower to the Lanthorn Tower. Indeed some of the foundations recently discovered by the Office, including the footings of the Lanthorn Tower and its adjoining chamber block, only served to demonstrate the correctness of their argument and the lack of justification for Taylor's scheme.

None of the points raised by the Society was properly addressed by the Office, which simply pressed ahead with its programme regardless of opposition. As far as the correspondence is concerned, the Society had the last word, their Secretary, Thackeray Turner, declaring prophetically on 3 March 1883 that his Committee

> ventures to predict that in a few years the views it now sets forth will be thought not popular yet so generally received by educated people that the notion of building a medieval Tower to show what England was like in the 13th century will finally be given up and in place of it a respect for genuine remains of former times will prevail.

During September 1885 the Record House and the adjoining storehouse were demolished and the construction of the curtain wall to the west of the Lanthorn Tower commenced. Work was completed in 1888. The reconstructed defences (**86**), with their 'crazy paving' stone faces and wall-walks carried on fanciful arcades, were built to an arbitrary design, on the wrong alignment and at the expense of what remained of the original medieval structure; not exactly an admirable achievement, but one which nevertheless contributed towards Taylor's subsequent knighthood. Ultimately, although the Society for the Protection of Ancient Buildings had won all the academic and ethical arguments, a blind, but determined, officialdom prevailed. Doubtless some of the stone from the remains of Henry III's chamber block was used as building rubble in

enabled him to 'state with certainty that the front of the [Record] House is not as ancient as stated in the letter of the Society'. He felt confident, therefore, that the line of the medieval curtain would be found 10ft north of the house frontage, that is, where his reconstruction plans had already placed it.

On 3 November the Office wrote to the Society informing them of Taylor's discoveries. The letter stated that the First Commissioner was of the opinion that the maintenance of the house was inconsistent with the works contemplated, that it would stand proud of the restored alignment and that all useful materials from the building would be preserved and employed in the new works. Since, however, there was such a wide difference of opinion between the Office and the Society as to the

86 *The late nineteenth-century Lanthorn Tower and curtain wall looking south-west* (photo: Garry Kennard, Royal Armouries).

the new structure, but nothing more is known about the promise to preserve the Record Office's coat of arms or the baroque panelling. Finally, an assurance by the Office to treat all archaeological remains with the greatest respect seems to have been forgotten when the area behind the new defences was terraced to make way for a concrete surface. The loss of part of this important archaeological record was made all the more pointless when, after a short period of time, the concrete was deemed rather unattractive and large quantities of soil were introduced to conceal it.

The last building erected in the nineteenth century, and also the last structure at the Tower to be designed in the gothic tradition, was the Main Guard building raised on the site of the earlier guard house to the north of the Wakefield Tower (**87**). This large three-storeyed building was constructed in brick and stone between December 1898 and July 1900 and contained in addition to the guard room, an

87 *The 1898–1900 Main Guard after being gutted by fire in October 1940* (English Heritage).

orderly room, office and stores, recreation area, mess and lecture rooms. The War Office's original estimate for construction was £16,361, the actual cost was £19,502.

13

Functions of the post-medieval castle

The Tower immediately after the Middle Ages continued to perform its primary role as a fortified palace. Henry VII was evidently not a frequent resident but he did create a second court to the east of the old palace complex. The relationship between the existing royal apartments and his new gallery and gardens, indicates a layout along the lines of the urban continental Burgundian model, with its emphasis on galleries intersecting gardens within the palace plan.

The demise of the royal lodgings

As the Tudor era advanced social and political changes, coupled with developments in the art of war, meant that the Tower and other royal palaces were increasingly rendered obsolete. The very physical form of the castle prevented any major modernization of the plan and the Tower became less and less a royal residence and more, as Holinshed put it, 'an armourie and house of munition, and thereunto a place for the safekeeping of offenders than a palace roiall for a king or queen to sojourne in'. Henry VIII was the last monarch to renovate and improve the ancient palace, with considerable works being undertaken in time for the coronation of Anne Boleyn in May 1533. Thereafter Henry rarely, if ever, came again, and Anne only for the trauma of her imprisonment and execution. The twilight of royal occupation had passed and with it the Tower effectively lost its medieval *raison d'être*.

For the government departments, the sixteenth century ushered in a period of expansion and with it additional demands on the available space within the Tower. Even before the coronation of Anne Boleyn, part of the royal lodgings had been encroached upon when the Wakefield Tower and its adjoining chamber block were converted into the nucleus of the Record Office at the Tower. As time went by the pressure to utilize the old palace buildings became irresistible. The next incursions evidently came early in the reign of Elizabeth I, with the construction of a silver refinery for the Mint somewhere in the palace grounds. At the same time the Ordnance acquired stores in 'the Queens chamber within her graces lodging' and by the end of the century had established an official storehouse within the palace ward (possibly Henry III's great hall). During the Interregnum the Ordnance converted Henry VIII's wardrobe range between the Broad Arrow and Wardrobe towers into a powder house.

The concept of the Tower as a royal residence, however, lingered on. Even after the Restoration the Office of Works resumed maintenance of some of the old palace buildings against the south face of the White Tower for possible royal occupation, but the practice was finally abandoned in 1668 as the Ordnance's reconstruction of the area began in earnest. The lodgings against the White Tower would not, in any event, have provided adequate accommodation for Charles II who made no use of them the evening before embarking on his traditional coronation procession from the Tower in April 1661.

The Tower as an arsenal

Of the various departments that operated within the Tower it was the Office of Ordnance which, until the second half of the nineteenth century, made the most territorial demands. The great surge in the Office's activities that preceded the Restoration was intended to modernize the Tower as a central depository for arms and ordnance and all manner of warlike stores. The Tower was by far the most important arsenal in the country 'almost your single Magazine' the Earl of Southampton advised the king in a letter dated 5 December 1663, while in December 1688 the future King William III, at least according to Sir Edward Sherburne, was more interested in securing the fortress than establishing a free Parliament. If Charles I had managed the same 46 years earlier the course of the Civil War might have been radically different. By the end of the seventeenth century, however, the Tower's military pre-eminence was beginning to wane as other establishments were developed and enlarged. It is perhaps not surprising that by this time, with Britain beginning to play the part of an imperial world power, a medieval castle in the centre of London was finding the task of supplying much of the needs of the army and navy increasingly difficult.

Perhaps one of the first signs that the leading role could no longer be sustained was the short-lived attempt during the 1660s to create a grand powder magazine within the White Tower. The supply route forged from the Wharf to the White Tower was abandoned in 1670, less than three years after it had been constructed. Only in 1667 did the amount of gunpowder stored in the White Tower come close to the 10,000 barrels envisaged. Thereafter the figure, with fluctuations, declined until the early eighteenth century, when approximately 600 barrels remained in the sub-crypt. Even then this relatively small amount proved troublesome to maintain, with the Mayor and Aldermen of London petitioning the Queen in 1706 in an effort to prevent the transportation of supplies through the streets of the City. There can be no doubt that the dispersal of powder to remoter magazines such as Upnor and Greenwich was in response to the threat that this highly volatile material posed to the City and the Tower. No incident demonstrated the danger more vividly than that of the morning of 9 July 1691 when the floor of the powder room collapsed, sending some 2000 barrels of powder crashing down on to the floor below.

When Charles I came to the throne the gun foundry at the Tower was probably still in existence, but not very active. By the time of the Restoration it had disappeared with most gun-founding now being carried out by private contractors operating in the southern counties.

For a few years the process of proving guns at the Tower seems to have continued. However, the tests were potentially hazardous, as evidenced by accounts for the repair of roofs etc, and after about 1670 the practice seems to have been discontinued. At this time the amount of heavy iron ordnance held in store also began to decline as depots such as Portsmouth, but particularly Greenwich, began to expand. Together with Chatham, the Tower remained the chief arsenal for brass artillery, though compared to iron guns, the demand for these pieces was relatively small.

During the eighteenth and nineteenth centuries the Tower remained an important depot for all manner of miscellaneous military stores, ranging from tents and cordage to grenades and swords. The French Wars that raged either side of 1800 saw the creation of an arms manufactory on the Wharf, which at the height of its activities seems to have had the potential to produce up to 50,000 guns a year. After the hostilities the Ordnance gunsmiths and furbishers returned to the traditional business of proving parts supplied by outside contractors.

Origins of the Ordnance Survey

An important, but little known, development in the Tower at the start of the reign of George I was the creation of the Ordnance Drawing Room, an establishment which was to make a notable contribution towards the training of British military surveyors and draughtsmen in the eighteenth century. During the seventeenth century the process of surveying and draughting within the Office was the preserve of the engineers who, according to their Instructions issued in 1683, were expected to 'draw and design the situation in any place, in their due Prospects, Uprights, and perspective'. In April 1712, however, a new chapter opened when the Board appointed one Robert Whitehead as a professional 'Draughtsman'. In July 1716 Andrews Jelfe, who three years later was to be appointed inaugural architect to the Ordnance, began preparing draughts and in January the following year he was joined by the highly talented Clement Lemprière. Lemprière's association with the Tower was to span nearly forty years and by 1741 he was Chief Draughtsman, with Desmartez as his deputy.

Significantly, the arrival of Jelfe and Lemprière was preceded by the decision in February 1716 to establish the Drawing Room on the first floor of the large stone building attached to the east side of the White Tower. Here the skills and reputation of the Drawing Room were to develop, culminating in the formation of the Ordnance Survey in 1791. The need for additional office space saw one of the great houses erected in 1699–1701 against the curtain wall opposite the Drawing Room being commandeered, and from here and their existing premises the draughtsmen continued to work until the Ordnance Survey moved to Southampton in 1841.

The fortifications and the garrison

Given the vital role the Tower played in the administration of Tudor and Stuart government it is perhaps surprising that little was done to improve the defences. The main obstacle to modernization must have been the various official departments which operated within the castle. It was of course the need for security that had seen these bodies evolve within the walls, but by the sixteenth century they had so crowded the confines of the castle that any major works on the defences would have meant a serious disruption of their activities.

Apart from some of the measures taken during the reign of Charles II in the wake of the Dutch raid on the Medway, most works to the defences were more concerned with combating internal threats, rather than any foreign incursion. In this respect the Tower could, and did, provide a base to suppress political opposition in the City. A permanent garrison, in the modern sense, evidently appeared during the Commonwealth, when as many as eight, but usually six, companies of the regiment raised by Colonel John Berkstead (the Parliamentary Governor of the Tower) were quartered there. The garrison was consolidated during the reign of Charles II, at which time purpose-built barracks were provided. Indeed the soldiers' lodgings erected in the Irish Mint in 1669–70 form one of the earliest known buildings of the type in the country. The military presence was further enlarged in 1682 when warrants were issued to '60 fed Gunners' who were required to lodge within the Tower and exercise as a company under the direction of the Master Gunner of England. This replaced an earlier, and evidently unsatisfactory, arrangement whereby 100 part-time gunners were relied upon.

During the reign of James II the offensive nature of the Tower was demonstrated when large mortars were planted on Legge's Mount and Brass Mount in an obvious attempt to intimidate the City, while part of the garrison was quartered on three London meeting-houses known to be frequented by persons 'disaffected' with the government. Detachments were often called upon to quell disturbances: a regiment was sent to break up a riot in Southwark in 1693, while four years later troops were dispatched to deal with trouble in Westminster, an hour's march away. Much closer at hand, the constable was ordered to suppress riots about the Tower in 1719. These outside duties were to continue for another two centuries with, for example, the garrison being required to give military aid at the Bank of England, the South Sea Company and the East India Company in 1722, and the Customs in 1733.

Towards the end of the eighteenth century the authorities became particularly concerned about the possibility of the Tower being stormed by radicals, and military reports on the defences from this time up to the middle of the nineteenth century are peppered with references to the dangers presented by the 'mob'. With the Duke of Wellington occupying the post of constable and the Chartists at their most active, the garrison reached its zenith. Shortly before the turn of the century, however, the threat of popular insurrections, real and imaginary, began to subside, a point illustrated by the decision of the Tower authorities in 1843 to convert the glacis, the open ground beyond the moat wall, into gardens.

The growth of tourism

The Tower as a tourist attraction can be traced back to Elizabethan times when foreign visitors first began to write about the curiosities they had seen during their visits. The Royal Menagerie and the two displays of armour known as the Line of Kings and the Spanish Armour (see p. 70) were among the earliest attractions. The practice of systematically exhibiting the Crown Jewels began immediately after the jewels were moved to the Martin Tower in 1669. In 1671 this very nearly resulted in the theft of the crown, orb and sceptre by Colonel Blood, aided and abetted by a woman posing as his wife. In the wake of this notorious incident the whole business of showing the jewels was placed on a more secure footing and to date no further attempt to steal them has been made. Beginning in 1696 the visitor could see the most spectacular attraction the Tower has ever had to offer – the Small Armoury arranged on the first floor of the Grand Storehouse by John Harris of Eton (see p. 71). Together with the historic ordnance housed on the ground floor below, this fabulous collection formed part, as Punch put it, of 'the enormous meal that fate had prepared' for a fire that began on the evening of 30 October 1841.

The 'great and awful conflagration' of 1841 failed, as did the Duke of Wellington's opposition to public admission and an Irish terrorist bomb in the White Tower on 24 January 1885, to prevent ever increasing numbers of visitors from coming to the Tower. By 1851 it was necessary to provide a purpose-built ticket office at the western entrance with public conveniences attached. A few years earlier the first official guidebook appeared, to challenge the private ones that had been available since about 1750. By the end of the nineteenth century visitors to the Tower numbered more than half a million a year.

Myth and misconception

Interest in the history and architecture of the Tower had been stimulated by the publication of John Bayley's great work, *The History and Antiquaries of the Tower of London,* in 1821, and to a lesser extent by the appearance of Britton and Brayley's excellent *Memoirs of the Tower of London* in 1830. It was, however, the appearance of Harrison Ainsworth's *The Tower of London, A Historical Romance* in 1840 which captured the greatest audience. According to this account, which in effect was the culmination of earlier tales, the Tower of London was some sort of ancient, mysterious place where famous and tragic personalities passed over cold stone floors on the way to the scaffold. Here were to be found the dungeons (a post-medieval corruption of the French word *donjon*, meaning great tower) in which miserable wretches awaited their fate (even though the Tower has virtually no basemented rooms, save those in the White Tower and behind the Chapel of St Peter). Readers were told of a time 'when Tower Hill boasted a scaffold, and its soil was dyed with the richest and best blood in the land', though it should be pointed out that public execution was unknown before the fourteenth century and only reached a sort of peak during the early modern era of the Tudors and Stuarts.

Like any castle in England, the Tower's role as a prison was incidental, being largely brought about by the close proximity of the royal courts at Westminster – thus it proved a secure and convenient place to hold prisoners of rank. This was particularly so during the religious and political upheavals of the sixteenth and seventeenth centuries; but even then it represented a minor ingredient in the daily life of the Tower when compared to the activities undertaken by the Mint and the Ordnance Office.

Courtesy of the historical novelist, however, the castle is assumed to have been erected solely for the incarceration, torment and eventual execution of the famous. Ainsworth and some of his contemporaries despised many of the seventeenth- and eighteenth-century buildings at the Tower, which must have reminded them of the great workshop and storehouse that they comprised, rather than a relic from a romantic England that never existed. To Ainsworth the Grand Storehouse (see **49**) was 'that frightfull structure' an 'ugly Dutch toy' which he hoped to see razed to the ground. The blaze that destroyed the building one year after he damned it in print must, therefore, have greeted him with jubilation.

The Tower in the second half of the nineteenth century ceased to be what it had been throughout the previous 700 years – a complex of buildings constantly adapting to meet the residential, military and administrative needs of its inhabitants and the people who worked there. Now it was cleared of all unworthy accretions and restored to the appearance of a building of the medieval age – an age whose architecture and social customs were only just beginning to be rediscovered. It is only with these considerations in mind that much of the present external appearance of the fortress can be appreciated. The tops of the walls bristle with regular crenellations whose impractical design no medieval builder would have embraced. The ragstone masonry of the reconstructed and resurfaced walls is so regimented, as in the case of the Devereux Tower, or so fancifully uncoursed, as with the Salt Tower, as to provide no comparison with the original. Moreover, many of the spaces between the curtain lines have been cleared of their structures to produce uncluttered, sterile vistas that could never have existed in former times. These views serve now to remind us of the aspirations of architects like Salvin and Taylor, men whose philosophy towards ancient buildings was itself to become history in the twentieth century.

14

The Tower in the twentieth century

After the hectic programme of restorations carried out during the Victorian era, works at the Tower during the twentieth century, with the notable exception of those brought about by damage during the Second World War, have been restrained and largely concerned with repair and consolidation. In 1905 part of the parapet on the east face of the Martin Tower was rebuilt in stone and three sash windows directly below replaced with medieval-style openings (see **80**). This exercise was intended to show how the tower would look if the various eighteenth-century brick linings and windows were replaced throughout. Thankfully the project was taken no further and the isolated stone crenellations that were formed now serve as a sort of monument to the last breath of the Victorian policy of recreation.

In 1908 the War Office reconstructed the rear wall of Brass Mount and during the following year plans to convert the core of the bastion into Warders' accommodation were prepared. In the event these came to nothing, but in 1914 the War Office carried out extensive works to convert the building into a store for 41,000 rifles previously housed on the ground floor of the White Tower. The operation necessitated the removal of the earth fill of the bastion to allow for the creation of three floors. It was during these excavations that the lower part of Edward I's curtain wall was uncovered; unfortunately the masonry was removed to enlarge the area of the basement.

In 1914 four large Victorian clock faces, together with the mechanism that operated them, were removed from the summit of the north-east turret of the White Tower (see **83**) and with the aid of early drawings the walls were restored. At the same time ambitious designs were drawn up for the excavation and flooding of the moat about the western entrance and the recasting and enlarging of Salvin's Engine House and Wharfinger's Cottage to the south, to form a large Tea House (**88**). The outbreak of the First World War, however, prevented further progress.

In the years that followed the War few significant works were carried out, though between 1925 and 1929 the Byward Tower attracted much attention. Various accretions against the rear of the tower were removed (**89**) and a good deal of the timber studwork exposed. Much of this was evidently never intended to be seen, and has proved difficult to maintain as well as presenting a very misleading picture. Serious consideration should be given to concealing this 'wealth of exposed beams', as the jargon goes, with a sympathetic coat of lime plaster.

Between 1934 and 1938 considerable works were in progress at the western entrance, though these represented a major revision of the plans prepared in 1913. The early Victorian Ticket Office was demolished and Salvin's Engine House extended northwards (by two bays) to form a ground-floor restaurant with offices above. During enabling works, part of the buried Lion Tower was discovered and this precipitated a major excavation to the north and north-west of the Middle Tower to reveal part of Edward I's moat, together with the two fine causeways and their bridge pits that provided access into the barbican from the east and north. These investigations, which were supervised by the eminent architectural historian John Harvey, were one of only a handful of archaeological investigations carried out at the Tower prior to the Second World War. The

88 *One of several artist's impressions prepared in 1913 for a Tea House at the Western Entrance* (English Heritage).

89 *A late Victorian photograph of the rear of the Byward Tower* (Royal Commission on Historic Monuments, England).

first controlled excavations had in fact taken place in 1904 after the Society of Antiquaries obtained permission to look for the continuation of the Roman city wall south of the Wardrobe Tower. They were unsuccessful, save for the discovery of a short stretch of the wall's flint and clay foundations immediately south of the Wardrobe Tower.

Whereas during the First World War the only bomb that fell on the Tower landed harmlessly in the moat, during the Second a number of buildings were seriously damaged or destroyed. The mid-nineteenth-century North Bastion, having narrowly avoided damage in September 1940 when a bomb fell in the moat, was blown apart on 5 October after receiving a direct hit (**90**). The late Victorian Main Guard was gutted by fire on 29/30 October 1940 (see **87**) while the northern part of the Old Hospital Block was taken down after sustaining serious structural damage (**91**). In the Outer Ward the former Master Assay Office of the Royal Mint was destroyed by a bomb on 23 September 1940 (**92**). During the restorations that followed the end of hostilities most of the damaged buildings were either repaired or reconstructed, though the North Bastion was never rebuilt in preference to restoring the line of the outer curtain wall. The shell of the Main Guard was also dismantled to allow the remains of Henry III's curtain wall to be exposed and consolidated. The last vestige of the War disappeared in 1959 when a large pillbox at the east end of the Wharf was demolished (**93**).

90 *The massive walls of the mid nineteenth-century North Bastion after being wrecked by an explosion on 5 October 1940* (English Heritage).

Between 1953 and 1956 a general repair of the plinth of the White Tower was put in hand, which saw the removal of various Victorian repairs and refacings. The operation resulted in a number of archaeological discoveries including, against the south-west corner, the foundations of Henry III's Coldharbour Gate which were exposed and consolidated for display. On the east side of the tower the discovery of a fragment of tessellated pavement resulted in a limited investigation to reveal the layout of part of the Roman residential building that stood here, together with the line of the Roman city defences. Further significant works were to be carried out within the White Tower during the 1960s and early 1970s including the repair of the principal roof and those of the four turrets, the reflooring and refurbishment of the Chapel and basement, and the construction of the wooden stairs against the south elevation to enable the original entrance to be brought

back into use for the first time in three hundred years. It might be added that the White Tower during the 1960s was the first building in the Tower to have the filth and grime washed from its walls. During the last 25 years the process has been extended to include most of the other buildings (**colour plate 12**) and it is difficult now to appreciate just how dirty the Tower once looked.

It is not the purpose of this book to catalogue in great detail the works undertaken at the Tower during the 1970s and 1980s. It should be emphasized, however, that the great increase in archaeological activity that accompanied these works has provided much new evidence about the building history of the fortress. The way in which the buildings and their contents are presented and explained has also been changing so that the general visitor might better enjoy and appreciate what he or she sees. Areas previously closed to the public have been opened up, notably the Wall Walk along the inner curtain defences, which in two phases during the late 1970s and early 1980s was opened from the Wakefield Tower to the Martin Tower. Sadly the Tower's historic setting has

91 *The Old Hospital Block was partly destroyed during an air raid in 1940* (English Heritage).

all but been destroyed on the landward side over the last thirty years, as older architecture has increasingly been replaced by large and unmemorable office blocks. Only the view across the river towards Southwark offers a feel for the scale and appearance of the former townscape, but look quickly, for this vista is soon to be occupied by another massive office complex designed in a 'Venetian' style. This seems to beg the question of whether the Venetians will ever allow an office development in the style of the Tower of London to be erected opposite the Doge's Palace?

As the Tower has developed as an historic monument of international importance the role of its institutions has declined to a state where, sadly, the traditional, non-tourist, functions of the fortress now seem to face extinction. As a military supply base the Tower has inevitably declined and at the time that this is being written serious consideration is being given to closing down the remaining depot at the Brass Mount. The military population has also dwindled to a small detachment retained only for guard duties. The last police role the garrison performed was in 1911 when a detachment assisted the civil authorities in dealing with

92 *The former Master Assay Office of the Mint reduced to rubble in September 1940* (English Heritage).

the famous Sidney Street siege in Stepney.

At a time when the number of soldiers quartered in the Tower has reached an all-time low, the ravens, who are counted among the strength of the garrison and thus receive ration allowances of meat and biscuit, have increased their strength from six to eight as a result of breeding within the walls. There is no record of this happening before and in an effort to assist the momentum special cages have been constructed on the green to the south-west of the White Tower. The compliment of Yeoman Warders, whose total has constantly fluctuated since the sixteenth century, have also been increased in recent years to a strength of 42. This has largely been in response to the open-ing up of additional areas to the public. Apart from their ceremonial functions, visitor-related duties now account for most of the Warder's working week – a far cry from the sixteenth and seventeenth centuries when the warding of state prisoners was the prime task.

As for the Tower as a state prison, that chapter concluded in grand style with the detention in the Queen's House of Hitler's Deputy, Rudolf Hess, for four days in May 1941. As a place of execution the Tower staged something of a comeback during the First World War with the execution of 11 German spies between November 1914 and April 1916. The first, Karl Lody, will go down in history as the first man to be executed at the Tower for 150 years. The last execution was that of Josef Jaboks, another German spy, who was led before a firing squad on 14 August 1941. All the executions were carried out in the miniature

117

93 *The most recent defences – a Second World War pillbox on the Wharf shortly before its demolition in 1959* (Historic Royal Palaces Agency).

rifle range, a prefabricated structure that stood in the Outer Ward against the curtain wall between the Martin Tower and Constables Tower. The Tower, with its long and intricate history, deserves to be remembered for more than the isolated and extreme events witnessed in this shed, and the removal of the structure in May 1969, before it could become a feature of morbid fascination, is surely one demolition that can be applauded.

Visiting the Tower

The Tower is very much a working monument and a surprisingly large number of people still live within its walls. This inevitably places restrictions on visitors wishing to explore the confines of the site. Access to the lower floor of the Bell Tower, therefore, can only be achieved by passage through the private residence of the Governor of the Tower, while only a handful of people have ever seen the unusual mid-thirteenth-century vault of the ground floor of the Devereux Tower, since it forms the ceiling of the resident Yeoman Warder's boiler room. That said, additional areas have been opened to the public during recent years and more are earmarked as part of the forward plans of the Historic Royal Palaces Agency, the official government body responsible for the administration of the Tower since October 1989. The Historic Royal Palaces Agency has also embarked on a programme of re-presentation so that the following summary of those areas open to public and what they contain is likely to need adjustment in the years to come.

The White Tower
The historic and architectural centre-piece of the castle. The public have access to all parts of the building except the roof. Apart from the splendid Chapel of St John, which is still used for periodic worship, the four floors form the heartland of the Royal Armouries Collection of historic arms and armour, including some of the finest and best known pieces, such as Henry VIII's armour.

The Medieval Palace
A new display will be opened to the public in 1993 explaining the history of the royal lodgings at the Tower. The exhibition encompasses the upper floors of the Lanthorn, Wakefield and St Thomas's towers. The Lanthorn Tower will be the starting point and therefore form the interpretation area. Beyond, the upper chamber of the Wakefield Tower and the eastern half of St Thomas's Tower will be sparsely furnished to provide an impression of how the rooms might have appeared during the reign of Edward I. The western half of St Thomas's Tower, which formed the king's innermost chamber, has undergone so many structural alterations as make its original form and appearance impossible to detect. The area will therefore be left as an 'archaeological zone' where the latter history of the building can be told.

The Wall Walk
A walk traverses the walls and towers of the eastern inner defences, beginning at the Salt Tower and ending at the Martin Tower. In the near future it is hoped to extend this to include the upper floors of the Brick, Bowyer and Flint towers along the northern curtain wall. At present the Salt Tower contains a small exhibition on the architecture of the building and prisoners at the Tower and the Broad Arrow Tower a notional representation of a late fourteenth-century knight's bedchamber while the uppermost floor of the Martin Tower features a collection of historic prints and engravings.

The Lower Martin Tower
The ground-floor chamber contains the Royal Armouries historic collection of instruments of torture.

The Beauchamp Tower
The ground and first floor are open to the public. The former features a computerized display on the history of the building while the upper chamber, famous for its collection of inscriptions carved on the walls, contains a tableau recording the imprisonment of Philip Howard, Earl of Arundel, during the reign of Elizabeth I.

The Bloody Tower
The tower has been furnished to evoke the occupation of Sir Walter Ralegh during the early years of the seventeenth century.

The New Armouries Building
Parts of the ground and first floors contain the Royal Armouries displays of British military history.

The Fusiliers Building
The former mid-nineteenth-century Officers' Block now houses the museum of the Royal Regiment of Fusiliers.

The Waterloo Block
The western half of the ground floor contains a prelude to the Crown Jewels comprising the plate and dress collection. The Jewels themselves are located in a vault below. By 1994 it is intended to have all the Regalia exhibited on the ground floor.

Chapel of St Peter ad Vincula
The church of the Tower and resting place of various famous individuals from English history. Though open to the public, entry is restricted to the tours provided by the Yeoman Warders.

Lower Cradle Tower
The original part of Edward III's private watergate.

Further reading

There is an enormous number of books written about the Tower of London and simply to list them in a standard bibliography would be tedious and unhelpful. A good deal of what is written is romantic, sensational and poorly researched, often simply rehearsing the views, and perpetuating the errors, of previous writers. The note below, therefore, is highly selective. Much of the documentary evidence for the later chapters of this book is taken from the extensive records of the War Office, Office of Works, Audit Office, Exchequer and Privy Council records held in the Public Record Office. Unfortunately limited space does not allow references to be quoted here.

General works
The first topographical and historical description of the Tower occurs in John Stow, *Survey of London* (1598 and subsequent editions). There is an important section on the Tower by William Maitland in *A History of London* (1739 and subsequent editions) which seems to have provided the basis for the first true guidebook: *An Historical Account of the Tower of London and its Curiosities* (*c*.1750) published annually with minor alterations until 1800. A major advance in scholarship came with John Bayley's *The History and Antiquaries of the Tower of London* (1821) in two volumes (single in 1830). This was supplemented by the excellent John Britton and E. W. Brayley, *Memoirs of the Tower of London* (1830). The subsequent spate of general histories contain little new information until the arrival of the commemorative volume that celebrated the notional 900th anniversary of the Tower: John Charlton (ed.), *The Tower of London: its Buildings and Institutions* (1977) which contains numerous interesting articles on the history of the Tower, its customs and traditions.

The architecture of the Tower
Most of the works listed above contain sections on the architecture. G. T. Clark, 'The Military Architecture of the Tower of London' in *Old London* (1867) is of seminal importance. See also A. W. Clapham, 'The Tower of London and its Development' in *Some Famous Buildings and their Story* (1912) and for a fuller description Royal Commission on Historical Monuments *London*, Vol. V (1930). The essential work on the documentation of the building is *The History of the King's Works*, Vols. I, II, III, and V (1963–76), while the most complete description of the architecture is in R. Allen-Brown and P. E. Curnow *The Tower of London*, Official Guidebook (1984). For an assessment of the Beauchamp Tower, its adjoining curtain walls and the early use of brick see P. E. Curnow 'Some Observations on the Planning and Construction of the West Curtain Wall at the Tower of London' in *Mélanges d'Archéologie et d'Historie Médiévales* (1982).

The archaeology of the Tower
The evidence for the Roman city defences and their subsequent adaptation in the medieval castle is found in G. Parnell, 'The Roman and Medieval Defences and the Later Development of the Inmost ward, Tower of London: Excavations 1955–77' in *Transactions of the London and Middlesex Archaeological Society* Vol. 36 (1985). For the early Norman defences see B. K. Davison, 'Excavations in the Tower of London' in *Château Gaillard*, Vol. 2 (1974) and G. Parnell, 'The Western Defences of the Inmost Ward, Tower of London' in Transac-

tions of the London and Middlesex Archaeological Society Vol. 34 (1983). There is an important report on the investigations in and about the Wakefield Tower by P. E. Curnow in *Ancient Monuments and their Interpretation*, edited by M. Apted *et al.* (1977).

Ordnance and Mint
The only specific articles on the Ordnance and the Mint at the Tower are by Sarah Barter in *The Tower of London: it's Buildings and Institutions*, John Charlton (ed.), 1977. There is some additional material on the Ordnance in H. L. Blackmore, *The Armouries of the Tower of London: The Ordnance* (1976) and (18) H. C. Tomlinson, *Guns and Government: The Ordnance Office under the later Stuarts* (1979). For the Mint see John Craig, *The Mint: a History of the London Mint from AD 278 to 1948* (1948).

Glossary

ashlar Squared blocks of stone laid in regular courses with fine vertical joints.

aumbry Cupboard or recess in a wall for sacramental vessels.

bailey Walled enclosure or courtyard of a castle.

barbican Outward extension of a gateway protecting the entrance from attack.

bastion Projection from the general outline of a fortress from which the ground before the wall or rampart is covered. From mid-sixteenth century they are generally four-sided in design.

batter Inclined slope of a wall.

berm Level space between the edge of a ditch and wall.

bomb vault Arched ceiling or roof constructed of brick or stone and designed to withstand the impact of artillery.

camp-shed A facing of piles and boarding along a river bank or the side of an embankment.

casemate Bomb-proof vault within a rampart providing an emplacement for a gun and/or accommodation for the garrison.

counterscarp Exterior slope of a revetment or ditch.

culvert Tunnelled drain for passage of water under ground.

cupola Small domed turret built upon a roof.

curtain wall Wall enclosing a castle or one of its parts.

donjon Keep or great tower.

escutcheon A shield for armorial bearings.

garderobe Latrine, normally discharging into a cess pit or through an outer wall into the moat or on to the berm.

glacis Sloping ground beyond moat or outworks.

imprest Money advanced on loan.

keep Great tower or donjon.

kneeller A projection of timber or stone designed to support.

mural gallery Gallery constructed within the thickness of a wall.

motte An artificial mound of earth forming the stronghold of an eleventh- or twelfth-century, castle.

nogging The use of brick, stone, etc, to infill the spaces between the uprights of a timber-framed building.

offset Point where the thickness of a wall changes horizontally.

pentice Lean-to building or covered passage or gallery.

pipe roll Annual roll of accounts rendered to the Exchequer by sheriffs and other royal bailiffs.

piscina Carved shallow basin in which sacred vessels are washed.

postern Small, secondary, door or gate.

quadrant ditch Ditch with the shape of a quarter of a circle.

quoins Dressed stone used to finish corners of building. Blocks of dressed stone used to bond a length of wall at regular, vertical, intervals are sometimes referred to as vertical quoins.

rampart Protective earth or stone wall surrounding a castle or fortress.

re-entrant Angle in a wall facing inwards, rather than outwards.

saltpetre Potassium nitrate used in manufacture of gunpowder.

sedilia Series of seats, often recessed in wall and with canopies, for use by clergy.

studwork Intermediate posts between the main members of a timber frame.

Index

127

INDEX